Climate as a Design Factor

1 Laboratorium, new edition

A series of volumes edited by:
Tina Unruh, Department of Architecture
Lucerne University of Applied Sciences and Arts –
School of Engineering and Architecture

Climate as a Design Factor

Architecture and Energy

Christian Hönger, Roman Brunner,
Urs-Peter Menti, Christoph Wieser

With articles by Roger Boltshauser,
Gion Caminada, Philippe Rahm and Sascha Roesler

Edited by Tina Unruh

Quart Publishers

Climate as a Design Factor
Architecture and Energy

Volume 1 of the series Laboratorium
Revised and extended new edition

Edited by: Tina Unruh, Department of Architecture
Lucerne University of Applied Sciences and Arts –
School of Engineering and Architecture

Articles by: Christian Hönger, Roman Brunner, Urs-Peter Menti,
Christoph Wieser, Roger Boltshauser, Gion Caminada,
Philippe Rahm, Sascha Roesler
Translation from German into English: Benjamin Liebelt, Berlin
Text editing: Uli Matthias Herres, Tina Unruh

Simulation: Zentrum für Integrale Gebäudetechnik,
Hochschule Luzern – Technik & Architektur
Christoph Stettler, Urs-Peter Menti, Dieter Lüthi
Serge Mattli, Iwan Plüss (1st edition)
Drawings processing (1st edition): Tao Bam, Janine Boog, Michaela Burri,
Cornelia Keller, Dominik Nachbur, Irene Widerkehr
Drawings in "Case Studies on Main Bodies": Sarah Federli
Cover illustration: Janine Boog, Rainer Vonäsch

Graphic design: Quart Publishers, Linus Wirz
Lithos: Printeria, Luzern
Printing: Freiburger Graphische Betriebe, Freiburg D

ISBN 978-3-03761-073-2

Original edition 2013: German (ISBN 978-3-03761-072-5)

Quart Verlag GmbH
Denkmalstrasse 2, CH-6006 Luzern
books@quart.ch, www.quart.ch

Foreword to the revised and expanded new edition

Four years have passed since the now sold out first edition of *Climate as a Design Factor* and three volumes in the *Laboratorium* series have been published since then. Following the first publication on climate, the focus turned to *Researching Architecture*. The third volume, *Spatial Thinking*, was dedicated to the relevance of materials. In 2014, the fourth volume will include studies on monument preservation and energy. So a great deal has happened since the first edition in terms of content, but despite all the changes, one thing has remained, was consolidated and could grow: the number and size of research projects that focus on aspects of materials, structure and energy in architecture. We can therefore fulfil the promise of continuity we made in our first edition, which is a great success for everyone involved.

This second edition not only gave us the chance to update data and integrate the latest insight, but also to take a look at the theme from the outside: Four competent colleagues are represented here with their very personal and therefore highly contrasting stances on *Climate as a Design Factor*. We wish to warmly thank them for their willingness to contribute their comment, thereby acting as examples that give readers a more precise understanding of the theme's broad range. We are also grateful to the School of Architecture and Engineering, the *Zentrum für Integrale Gebäudetechnik* and the Department of Architecture at the Lucerne University of Applied Sciences and Arts, which have provided financial support, as well as the sponsors named at the end of the book. They have all helped to publish this book both in German and English.

However a second edition would not have been possible without the great enthusiasm and passionate commitment that the authors from the different fields have once again invested into this new edition. We hope that the book's target readership – which still includes everyone who contributes to the creation of well-considered buildings – is inspired by that commitment and hence by this edition of *Climate as a Design Factor*.

Tina Unruh, Lucerne 2013

Climate and Architecture

Christian Hönger

Climate is described as the dynamic cycle of weather at a specific location that is repeated on a daily or annual basis. Global weather can be subdivided into various climate zones, for instance the tropics, sub-tropics, temperate zones, sub-polar and polar zones. The much-debated phenomenon of global warming caused by mankind will lead to a shift in climate zones in the coming decades. We are shaped by our climate, directly and indirectly, very early in life: be it by physiological experiences during early childhood, through the very different food we eat depending on the climate, and through the climate-imbued culture, represented by what we "inherit" from our forefathers. The term temperature is etymologically related to the word temperament, which expresses the nature of people in an energetic sense.[1] Climate shapes our environment. It is not surprising that autochthonous buildings in the temperate alpine zone of Bhutan resemble houses in our own Alps, despite the lack of cultural transfer between the regions. However, the term climate is also applied to interior spaces. A good interior climate is characterised by low pollutant levels and sufficient air exchange. A broader sense of the word not only takes physical values into account, but also atmospheric aspects such as effects and moods.

Today, "looking after the environment" means leaving the path of Modernism, during which architecture was imposed upon its environment in a colonialistic way. The task now is far more to think one's way into an environment and enter into a relationship with the location.

The principle discipline of architecture is to design. That involves anticipating a propective building in a complex conceptual and planning process. Classic design factors are utilization, space, construction and form, dependent on time and location.[2] The location – which

[1] Tetsuro Watsuji even speaks of climatic human types, in: Watsuji 1992

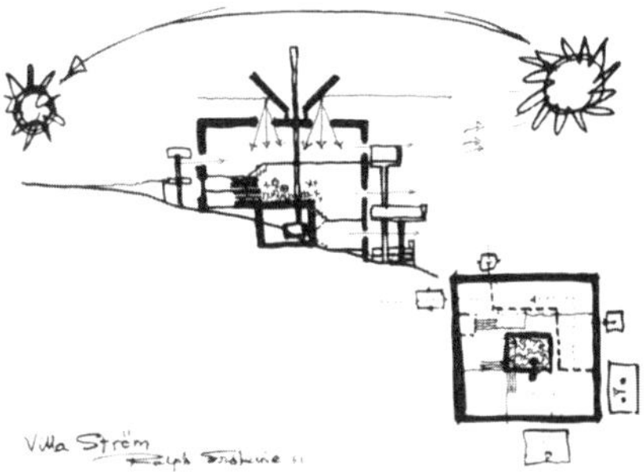

Ralph Erskine: Villa Ström in Stocksund, 1961. In: Mats Egelius, Ralph Erskine, arkitekt, 1988, Stockholm. p. 57

has after Modernism again become an important factor of design – was introduced by Christian Norberg-Schulz with the term *genius loci*.[3] It equally includes the historic substance, knowledge, memory, perception, aura and atmosphere. Climate is not mentioned as an influencing factor in this context.

Nevertheless one could figuratively compare design to cooking: If something is not listed in the recipe, it will not be bought and cannot therefore become an integral part of a menu. In other words, what is not acquired from the very beginning cannot be subsequently integrated. So if the climate is not part of the early design phase, it will not influence dominant factors such as form and typology and will require subsequent technical means in or on the building to compensate.

The book's title "Climate as a Design Factor" is therefore a manifesto as well: It concisely states that climate is a decisive physical factor and must be integrated into the early design process!

[2] Hoesli 1989. p. 31

[3] Norberg-Schulz 1982

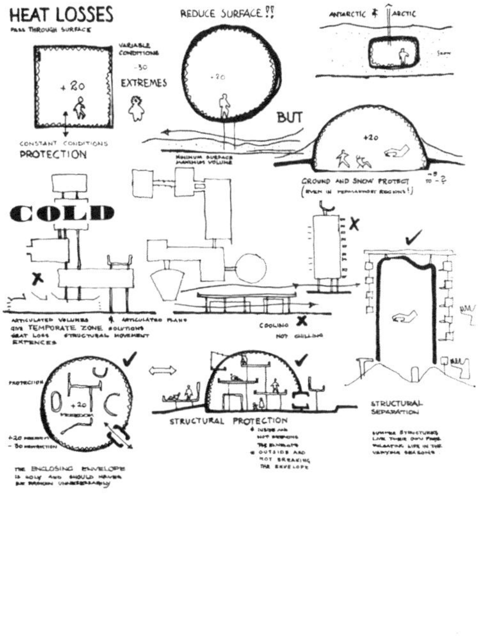

Ralph Erskine: Minimising the building surface and preventing façade perforation to reduce heat loss. Study: "The Sub-Arctic Habitat", 1959. In: Oscar Newman, CIAM '59 in Otterlo, 1961, Stuttgart. p. 164

Thesis

Christian Hönger, Roman Brunner

The energy problem is widely debated today. Much is talked about the industrialised world's dependency on limited supplies of non-renewable energy sources, most often combined with calls for new technologies. Certainly, technology is hailed as a response, be it highly developed or alternative. At least that is the consistent claim by politicians and opinion leaders. It is known that buildings around the world consume the most resources and produce large amounts of pollutants. Relatively little in terms of concrete statements on the subject is heard from architects themselves, although they could regard the theme as a challenge. The question of how architecture is able to minimise energy consumption is hardly investigated or discussed within the profession itself. This publication attempts to take on this as yet unattractive theme and grasp it as a chance. The 1973 oil crisis revealed how limited fossil fuels are and how much the western world's economic well-being depends on them. As a result, alternative fuels were sought, buildings were insulated and more efficient technologies were developed. Although a report ordered by the Club of Rome stressed the limits of growth and the effects of industrialisation as early as in 1972, the problem only entered into public consciousness twenty years later at the Rio de Janeiro Earth Summit in 1992.[1] So the foresight of Buckminster Fuller's Dymaxion map, which was produced in 1940, is all the greater, since it was so early in communicating the wasteful way in which energy was being consumed. His charts highlighted the contrasting situation vividly. Even at the time, the difference between the consumption of energy in industrialised and developing countries was obvious, as industrialised countries consumed 75% of all energy, but made up only 25% of the world population.

Despite the early warnings, the global problem has worsened. Non-renewable resources will be completely consumed in the foreseeable future. Industrialised society has caused an acute pollution problem and is forced to cope with global warming and its consequences.

[1] The Limits to Growth is a study on the future of the global economy published in 1972. Contracted by the Club of Rome, Donella and Dennis Meadows and their colleagues at the W. Forrester Institute for Systems Dynamics produced a system analysis with a calculation model that took the high degree of networking in global processes into account and allowed computer simulations on different scenarios. The report's central conclusions postulate that in the case of unchanged increases in the world population, industrialisation, environmental pollution, food production and the exploitation of natural resources, absolute growth limits on earth would be reached in the following hundred years.

[2] Behling 2000. p. 20

[3] Schwarz 2007. p. 600

[4] Metz 2006. p. 502

[5] The economist Ernst Friedrich Schumacher proclaimed a similar world view in 1979.

[6] Nikolaus Kuhnert writes in his article "Moderne und Tradition": "The present age is dominated by two essentially different building philosophies: The building philosophy of Modernism and the building philosophy of a reborn tradition. (…) In that sense, the works by Hassan Fathy are characteristic of the building philosophy of a renewed tradition." Fathy 1987. p. 30 [trans.]

Half of all energy is consumed by buildings,[2] while at the same time almost 40% of the life-cycle costs of buildings could be saved.[3] That results in a great responsibility in the building industry and for architecture. Sustainability and the sparing use of non-renewable energy have become a necessity and could become an inspirational challenge for architects, building technology engineers and construction physicists.

The dominant world view of the key industrial nations is characterised by a capitalist, highly industrialised world order that has in fact achieved its supremacy by exploiting fossil fuels. Coal, oil and gas are joined by energy carriers such as nuclear power and fusion, which continue to be in use and receive funding.[4] Such a world view is based on constant growth with the mission of mass production and global concentration processes in major cities. Technology and high technology are in this context both trusted means and desirable

[7] Cf. publication and exhibition: International Style by Philip C. Johnson and Henry-Russell Hitchcock in 1932 at the MOMA: The International Style: Architecture Since 1922, and the standard work on Modernism: Space, Time & Architecture, published in 1941 by Siegfried Giedion. In both cases, none of the architects named here were represented.

[8] With respect to architecture, the term is characterised by the publication by Norberg-Schulz, 1982

[9] See among others: Der Triumph des Mockens. Wie energieeffizientes Bauen das Bild der Städte verändern wird. In: Neue Zürcher Zeitung, 25. Juni 2009. p. 17

[10] Krausse: "The house therefore develops from a machine paradigm to an organic paradigm" In: ARCH+ Nr. 126 (Solare Architektur). Aachen 1995. p. 23 [trans.]

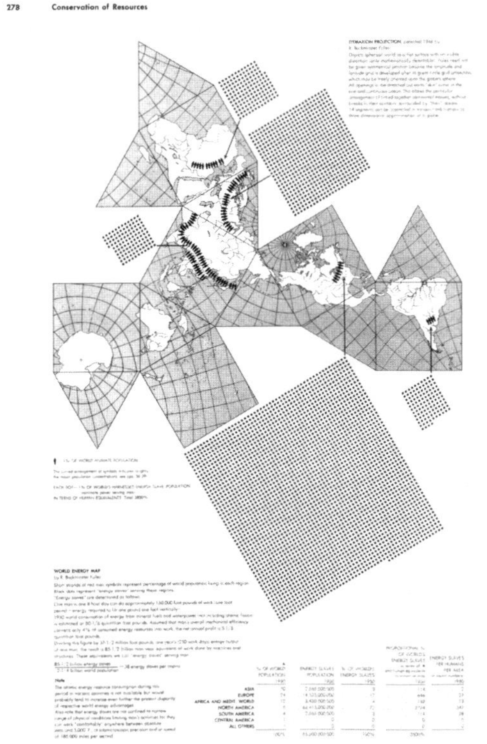

Herbert Bayer: World energy map in the World Geo-Graphic Atlas, using the Dymaxion world map, 1953. In: Your Private Sky – R. Buckminster Fuller, 1999, Baden. p. 271
© Image archive, ETH Library, Zurich

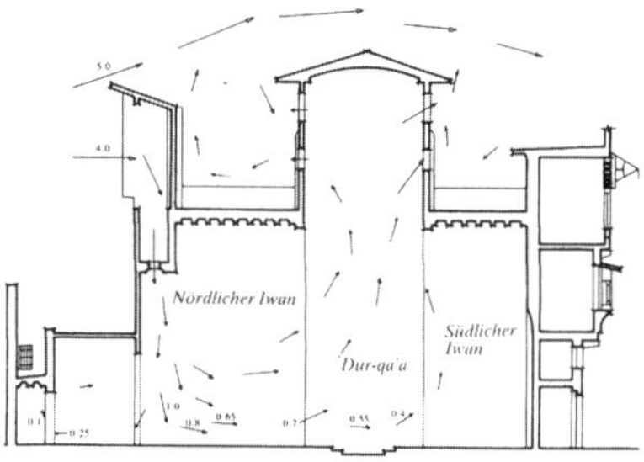

Hassan Fathy: Qa'a of the Muhib Ad-Din Ash-Shaf i Al-Mawaqqi, Cairo, 1350. In: Arch+ Feb. 1987, Aachen. p. 43

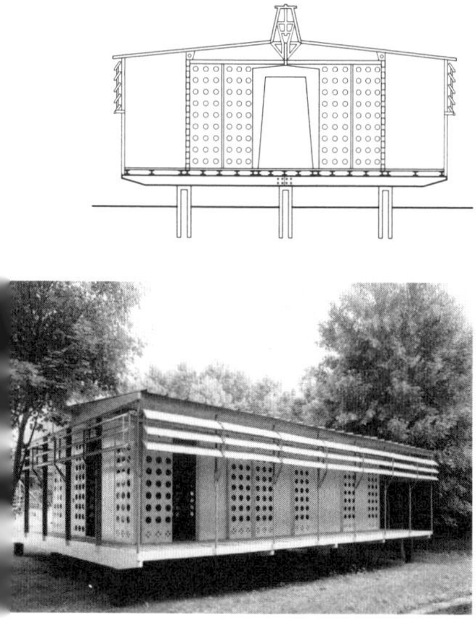

Jean Prouvé: Maison tropique, photo and sectional view, 1951. In: CW-Volume 3, p. 32

images and symbols of future progress, as pretended by science fiction films such as Star Wars or Blade Runner. Renewable energy resources are a rather insignificant footnote in the face of such a dominant world view. Today's global architecture is akin to that view. Oriented towards an "architecture of the international stars", which mainly focuses on highly industrialised, capitalist civilisations, it stands for an international or multicultural style that can be applied everywhere and adapted to the local conditions by using technical means.

The alternative is a different world view that already existed before industrialisation and developed out of the local, social and climatic conditions of a place. People erecting buildings with this perspective regard both the sparing use of resources and a minimised utilization of technical means to be self-evident. The key concept of endlessly growing productivity is fundamentally questioned here, shifting the focus toward an end of high technology. Renewable energies are radically supported and encouraged.[5] That understanding includes the equal distribution of economic power and a revaluation of labour. It is a different world view that concurs with an architecture that scientifically investigates the local climatic conditions, analyses and empirically assesses the local building culture and transforms it in contemporary design – not in the sense of copying the picturesque in regional buildings, but in the sense of a "renewed tradition".[6] Overshadowed by Modernism[7] – and entirely ignored by it – the inspirational protagonists of such a view have taken their own paths. With their stances, statements and buildings, these architects and pioneers born between 1880 and 1922 are also the spiritual patrons of this book. Between 1957 and 1962, Hassan Fathy (1900–1989) taught on the subject of climate and architecture as a Lecturer at the Athens Technical Institute. His concept of a renewed tradition is based on Egyptian-Arab thought and newly combines traditional clay building and classical typologies such as the courtyard and dome, while also integrating the aspect of of community. In his publication The Architecture of the Well-Tempered Climate, which was first published in 1969, Reyner Banham (1922–1988) distilled three clearly described approaches in handling the climate: the conservative, the selective and the regenerative method, which were each

appropriate for different climate zones, but are only partially effective when combined. Richard Buckminster Fuller (1895–1983) developed domes of a completely different kind to prevent what he called "cosmic bankruptcy". With his 1961 slogan "Think global – act local", the architect made a plea for "spaceship Earth", as well as for an energy-efficient, light, ephemeral architecture that placed minimal material demands. In 1964, Bernard Rudofsky presented the sense and beauty of autochthonous building forms with his provocative MOMA exhibition "Architecture without Architects". He expanded architecture and the contextual reference to include the sensory experience of architecture as well as the way of living: "Architecture is not just a question of technology and aesthetics, but also a framework for an – ideally viable – lifestyle." He is therefore spiritually akin to the Greek architect Aris Konstantinidis (1913–1993), who described buildings as "containers of life", which he rooted in the Greek landscape because of the shady zones between the interior and exterior and a traditional choice of materials. The connection between the climate and lifestyles was studied and described by the German architect and teacher Bruno Taut (1880–1938) in his book "Das japanische Haus und sein Leben" ("The Japanese House and its Life"), which was published in 1936. Taut lived in Japan between 1933 and 1936 and had by then begun to write his architectural thoughts, which were published in Turkish in 1938. In the chapter on technology, he writes: "There is no greater nonsense than the words of Le Corbusier: 'One will build the same way high up in the north and on the Mediterranean coast.' It is architecture's greatest possible infection by the bacillus of engineering."
In addition to those spiritual patrons, there have been practising architects who designed and erected buildings from a similar perspective. Equally overlooked by Modernism, architects such as Rifat Chadiriji in Iraq, Charles Correa in India, Geoffrey Bawa in Sri Lanka and Keck & Keck in the USA, as well as Louis I. Kahn, the late Le Corbusier in India or Jean Prouvé in Africa, all worked in accordance with that world view. Contemporary architecture also has such exponents, such as Gion Caminada in the Grisons region, the young architects Ivica Brnic, Florian Graf and Wolfgang Rossbauer

Le Corbusier: Tour d'ombre, Chandigarh/India, 1950. In: Daidalos 6/97, Berlin. p. 30

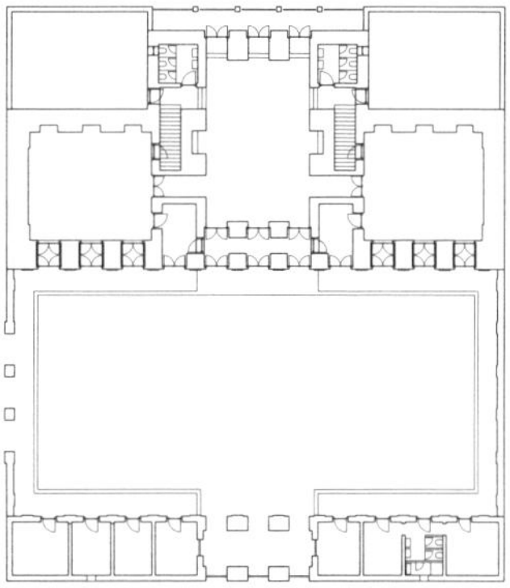

Ivica Brnic, Florian Graf and Wolfgang Rossbauer: ETH House of Science, ground plan, Bamiyan, Afghanistan, 2006

with their ETH House of Science in Bamiyan/Afghanistan or Studio Mumbai in India, to mention just a few representatives of this approach. To grasp sustainability in a holistic sense always includes the integration of the local climate and the reinterpretation of regional values, cultures and working methods.
To this day, architects mainly understand the location as living space, and the landscape and local building culture in the sense of the genius loci.[8] The focus lies on morphological or typological studies as well as a stance that defines the quality of architecture based on its relationship to its context. However, scientific study of the climate as a precondition for a locally specific design is hardly addressed in training and practice. Very simple facts are far too often overlooked: that the consumption of energy in buildings has a direct connection to the local climate. And moreover, that the requirements of the morphology, typology and materials of a highly energy-saving building mean it is quite possible it will not fit into the character of the existing buildings.[9]
Since Modernism, technology has been regarded as an essential condition for progress, and also as a symbol of open-mindedness, or even revered as a fetish.[10] Scientific perfectionism is valued much more highly thanthan pragmatic appropriateness. Sustainability itself is therefore mainly defined as a technical problem.[11] From that perspective, building becomes a mere "tuning" in the sense of a secondary vitalisation of a standard building, like those that can be seen everywhere and which continue to be built as a matter of course.[12]
Rooftop solar panels and heat pumps in the cellar are regarded as insignia of enlightened environmental awareness and used as a universal cure for guilty consciences. In view of the precarious situation, the building industry tends towards hasty and mainly technically motivated solutions – without any design ambition or aesthetic sustainability.[13] In Switzerland, two physical models are currently being discussed with respect to energy and architecture: Energy-savings (target: 2,000 Watt/person/year)[14] and minimising pollution (target: 1t CO_2/person/year).[15] In principle, both concepts are aimed at reducing pollution, especially when only "clean energy"[16] is used to implement them. The aim of greater autonomy with respect to the energy supply is desirable in both cases.

[11] The term "culture" is either completely lacking or only marginal in the definition of sustainability.
[12] Design is not integrated into the fields of the "Minergie-P-Eco" and "SIA Energy Efficiency Guildeline" standards.
[13] Georg Mörsch, Emeritus Professor for Monument Preservation, concisely describes the phenomenon he calls "protecting aesthetic integrity": "The building measures that are convincingly aimed at energy savings and – in congenial interaction with it – serve to support the appropriate industry – often starkly fall short of all standards relating to architectural and artisan culture. One should not speak of mere questions of taste, but instead of the loss of a building culture that has grown over centuries, which is a general quality of our environment. And as always, when one speaks of architecture as a sustainable, environmental task, it will in future continue to be only the aim and result of long-term, creative, ecological, artisanal and sustainable economic efforts." Mörsch 2008. p. 31 [trans.]
[14] Spreng, Semadeni 2001
[15] ETH Kompetenzzentrum Energy Science Center ESC and Prof. Dr. Hansjürg Leibundgut: Wegbeschreibung für Gebäude in eine nachhaltige Energie-Zukunft. Zurich, Institut für Hochbautechnik (Version 2.1) 2007

Mies van der Rohe: Neue Nationalgalerie, Berlin, 1962–68. In: Mies in Berlin. Ludwig Mies van der Rohe. Die Berliner Jahre 1907–1938. Munich/London/New York, 2001. p. 359

Architecture itself continues to be defined in teaching as the original organisation of space, its proportions and the highest aesthetic standards. Mies van der Rohe's *Neue Nationalgalerie* in Berlin, which is rightly celebrated in college lectures on Architecture as a timeless classic, is questionable from today's perspective of consuming resources and can thus no longer be regarded as an ideal worth striving for. The International Style[17] was an early example of architectural production that applied a universal, global style, and similar developments can be seen in buildings by so-called star architects today.

According to that understanding of architecture, technology is a compensator between climate and comfort demands: The architect delegates technical problems to specialists. However, building technology engineers must urgently develop an extended view of the cultural relevance of energy and sustainability in the sense of "systems engineers".[18] For their part, architects must work to understand the scientific and physical interrelationships of their designs.[19] An interdisciplinary view can produce a new architecture and a new understanding both of technology and extended professional roles.[20]

It should be examined whether climate and energy could develop into a primary design generator in addition to classic influencing factors such as the urban planning *gestalt* and typological organisation. The problem of energy and resources poses an underlying question to architects: How do we want to live?[21] How can we make ourselves comfortable without doing so at the expense of future generations? An answer to that fundamental question must have effects on our constructed environment. The following chapters in this book show how this could absolutely go hand in hand with a conscious perception and an increased quality of life.

The earliest strategic design phases define the underlying parameters of a building, which determine its perceived value, its operational feasibility and its lifespan. Due to growing economic and temporal pressure on planning and the production of buildings, that important early stage is often shortened in terms of time and funds, even if its effects are increasingly relevant to society as a whole. There is hardly time for in-depth study on new, morphological and typological inventions and these are not funded, which encourages a reversion to

[16] Clean energy means energy that has at least a 50% proportion of renewable resources (bioenergy, solar power, wind and hydroelectric power, as well as geothermal energy) and a maximum 50% proportion produced by climate-protecting, efficient combined heat and power plants based on gas (no nuclear power). The composition and source of the electricity must be clearly presented.

[17] Johnson, Hitchcock 1932

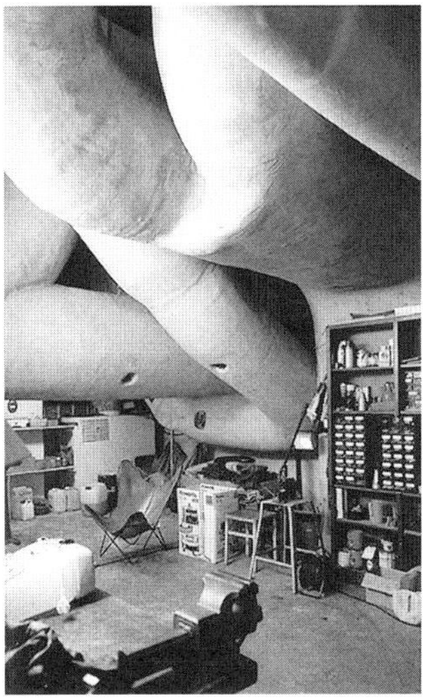

Mies van der Rohe: Neue Nationalgalerie, basement, Berlin, 1968. In: Lecture by Sebastian El Kouhli, MA course "Focus: Energy", winter semester 2007, Lucerne University of Applied Sciences and Arts – Engineering & Architecture

architectural déjà-vus. In today's standard planning process, the fundamental decisions with respect to the appearance and typology of architecture are made at an early design stage, mostly by the architects alone.[22] These decisions, with their leverage in terms of spatially effective resources and energy optimization – as well as the building form, orientation, typology and opening behaviour – are thereby already fixed even before the overall system of climate and technology can (re)act. Only in a subsequent step does the engineer develop the technology for the design and optimize it on that basis. Feedback to the original architectural design is generally impossible because its content has already been consolidated or politically determined in a competition, a preliminary study or project. To be able to develop such fundamental decisions at the right time, the chronological sequence of architecture and technology should be transformed into an interdisciplinary parallel process at the earliest design stage, whereby the term "technology" should be redefined and rather be regarded as a source of inspiration for architecture instead of a universal remedy. Logically therefore, the fee for the inspirational building services engineer should no longer be calculated on the basis of the sum of the installed technology, since he is involved from the outset. Instead, it should be measured with respect to the intelligence and suitability of the proposed solution.

How can we architects and planners come to our senses? By reminding ourselves of the primary elements of a location: seasons, sun, wind, rain and snow. The main components of architecture – form and space – are then not merely geometric, but also physical and physiological values. We should study them patiently and precisely, and experience them physically. Nature can act as an example for us: In nature, almost all organs developed for survival are not monofunctional, but efficiently assume several tasks. In architecture too, insight on analogous processes of selection and constant adaptation in autochthonous building forms were developed continuously. Due to the limited availability of resources and materials, the basic elements of architecture with respect to form and space had to be developed multifunctionally and self-sufficiently.

This publication seeks spatial-architectural, rather than technological, answers to the question of climate and energy. They are described

[18] The term "systems engineering" introduced around 1970 stems from the pioneering field of high-tech, namely astronautics. Systems engineering is the application of technical, scientific methods in order to develop the entire life cycle of a system in individual process steps, such as definition, synthesis analysis, design, integration, testing and proving, and to adapt all physical, functional and process-dependent interfaces to each other, so that the entire system and its implementation is optimised in interdisciplinary cooperation. Additionally, parameters such as reliability, maintainability, functional security and survivability, including disposal and operating functions are incorporated according to the given cost and time limits.

[19] "Energy turnover is basically organised in the house or through the house. This requires the controlled handling of locally available energy. Unfortunately, the connected questions have been passed on to specialist engineers and it is standard procedure to incorporate their solution into the architectural design only at a subsequent stage." Krausse 1995. p. 22 [trans.]

[20] Richard Buckminster Fuller was an early and vehement advocate of an interdisciplinary approach: "So, planners, architects and engineers, take the initiative. Go to work and above all, work together and keep no secrets from each other. Try not to gain at the expense of others (...)." Krausse 2008. p. 119 [trans.]

[21] Cf. Bernard Rudofsky (as a subheader to Sparta/Sybaris): "Instead of a new building method, a new way of living is required." [trans.] Österreichisches Museum für angewandte Kunst (Ed.), Residenz Verlag, Salzburg and Vienna 1987

[22] One exception to this is the practice currently being established in Switzerland of integrating construction engineers into the earliest design stage to develop a load-bearing structure that determines the appearance and form.

using different strategies and presented with examples. The presented strategies are explicitly reckoned as tools for architects and planners during the design process. The perspective is descriptive and spatial, rather than abstract and technical, since it is consciously aimed at stimulating the search for inspiring solutions. The introduced strategies are simulated, scientifically assessed and commented on with respect to their efficiency.

While buildings used to be optimized on the basis of a long chain of experience and conclusions in a trial-and-error method, such complex circumstances can be grasped today in simulations. The high-tech process of simulations can be used as condensed, accelerated experience to question hasty, automatised action and analyse a problem subjectively. By evaluating already existing buildings and spaces, simulations can accompany the architectural design process in an interdisciplinary way even during an early sketchy stage. Important design decisions on the appearance, typology and opening behaviour, as well as construction and materials, can now be extended to include the aspects of "climate" and "energy". Instead of being a helping mechanism that is retrospectively installed into the architecture, technology becomes a partner discipline on the path to an intelligent solution. Architecture can therefore achieve a reconquest: integrating high-technology into the design to allow the development of low-tech buildings. The result is an architecture that is sustainable in the long term and affordable worldwide.

Irina Mastel, Julian Wittwer: Tighremt. In: "Der Tighremt unter den Gesichtspunkten der Energie und Nachhaltigkeit", 2007/2008, Lucerne. p. 8

Diagram of varying use, Tighremt. p. 14

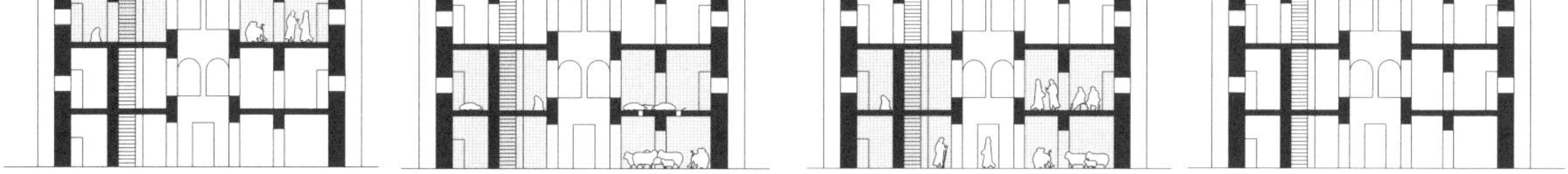

Winter day Winter night Summer day Summer night

Sascha Roesler – Climate and Culture

In terms of the history of civilisation, if there is a central source of knowledge for "climate-related" building, it lies in the field of everyday, domestic construction, which is known today as "traditional", "vernacular" or "informal" building. Accordingly, climate-related architectural research relies on the knowledge derived from builders all around the world, as manifested in the buildings and building practices they have developed. However, since this is non-theoretical, experience-based knowledge, we require empirical (ethnographic) studies by architects and ethnographers for the field of architecture to access this form of construction.[1] I assume that ethnographic research can provide architecture with access to insight that is relevant to the climate and cannot be acquired in a different way – for instance through experiment, simulation and calculation in research and development departments of technical colleges and the construction industry. Ethnographic and technological research on the climate must be mutually informative; climate-related architectural research must also be based on the ethnography of everyday domestic buildings.[2] This accessing of vernacular, informal buildings helps us replace our technology-minded consideration of the climate with a broader-based approach.

To turn the influencing factor of climate into a design factor in the first place, one must accept the idea that over the millennia, people have observed the natural environment in which they built. Many everyday domestic building methods around the world can be regarded as the evolutionary result of observing the climate. There is a provable, albeit rarely explicit correlation between climate zones and construction principles. People integrated themselves and their building methods into the local climatic conditions; but they also tried to manipulate them to their advantage using appropriate structural measures. That is the ambivalent aspect of adaptation to and adoption of natural conditions through construction and buildings.

Architecture should return to a dialogue with the climate, having simply negated it with its structural concepts in the 20th century. Today's architecture can be inspired and guided by the advance of thousands of years of traditional building. It can also reach new, optimized building solutions by itself observing nature and developing traditional building further. It remains to be seen whether that approach can quickly develop building elements such as the traditional Iranian wind screens (Bagdir), where the thermodynamic effect and architectural expression have achieved

[1] For the scientific history of ethnographic research on modern architecture, see: Roesler, Sascha: Weltkonstruktion. Der aussereuropäische Hausbau und die moderne Architektur. Ein Wissensinventar, Berlin 2013

[2] Examples of ethnographically informed climate research in modern architecture: Fry, Maxwell / Drew, Jane: Tropical Architecture in the Humid Zone, New York 1956; Fitch, J. M. / Branch D. P.: Primitive Architecture and Climate, in: Scientific American, 203, December 1960, p. 134–144; Olgyay, Victor / Olgyay, Aladar: Design with Climate – Bioclimatic Approach to Architectural Regionalism, New York 1992 (1963); Rapoport, Amos: House, Form and Culture, New York 1969; Givoni, B.: Man, Climate and Architecture, London 1981 (1969); Steadman, Philip: Energy, Environment and Building, Cambridge University Press 1975; Faskel, Bernd: Die Alten bauten besser – Energiesparen durch klimabewusste Architektur. Was für unsere Ahnen selbstverständlich war, müssen wir neu entdecken, Frankfurt am Main 1982; Turan, Mete (Ed.): Vernacular Architecture – Paradigms of Environmental Response, Aldershot 1990

congruence. But on that search, today's architects should not be discouraged by the fact that the connection between the climate and architecture is open and accordingly primarily symbolic and less physical. The "style-forming" effect of the climate[3] can often be seen less in provable physical evidence than in symbolic gestures, such as the expressive overhanging gabled roofs of the Sa'dan Toraja in Sulawesi (Indonesia). The roofs' function of weather protection has long transformed into the seat of the gods.[4]

Our fixation on the energy dimension of the climate has no relevance for worldwide vernacular and informal building. One important gain from ethnographic research in architecture is an understanding of the climate going beyond the dimension of energy.

What is far more necessary is a cultural-technical research that grasps architectural approaches to climatic conditions as a holistic cultural practice, in which buildings, clothing, physical behaviour and rituals are equally involved. What architects can study on everyday domestic buildings are actually cultures of climate conditioning that cannot be sufficiently defined by the term "low-tech". A vernacular, informal understanding of climate conditioning is always based on the interaction between the technology of buildings and techniques of the body, of building methods and lifestyles. It is known that in many places around the world, people change their location depending on the time of year and day; those locations are also insulated and heated to a different degree. If we want to move away from today's drab, global interior standard (20°C air temperature, 50% relative humidity), the everyday house that remains untouched by architects offers a wealth of study material thanks to its wide range of varieties: In the words of Ossip Mandelstam, "every room has its own climate."[5]

My focus on research (rather than design) allows me to avoid certain practical constraints that are imposed upon architectural offices. I see my privilege as a researching architect to lie in the ability to study and question structural "logics" that are presumed as "given" in daily practice. Fundamental research in architecture means developing new structural logics.

In my research, teaching and exhibition work, one of my aims is to make the idea of construction accessible again to architecture with respect to climate-related tasks. Construction as it is understood by architects and taught in colleges today is dominated by the field of (construction engineers') thought on the load-bearing structure. Industrialisation has turned construction into a quasi structure-forming science of architecture

[3] Bruno Taut referred to this aspect in 1937: "Everywhere around the world, in all zones and countries, the climate has dictated a fundamental, technical order, not only in windows, but in all parts of a building. Technical aspects modestly and carefully followed the demands of nature and formed the basis of style." In: Taut, Bruno: Architekturlehre – Grundlagen, Theorie und Kritik aus der Sicht eines sozialistischen Architekten, Beziehung zu den anderen Künsten und zur Gesellschaft, Istanbul 1937 / Hamburg 1977, p. 73 [trans.]

[4] See: Domenig, Gaudenz: Tektonik im primitiven Dachbau. Materialien und Rekonstruktionen zum Phänomen der auskragenden Giebel an alten Dachformen Ostasiens, Südostasiens und Ozeaniens. Ein architekturtheoretischer und bauethnologischer Versuch, ETH Zurich 1980

[5] See: Mandelstam, Ossip: Die Reise nach Armenien, Frankfurt am Main 1983 (Russian orig. 1934)

that seeks the expressive potential of the load-bearing structure. To break through that conceptual horizon, I believe an approach is necessary that changes both the discursive and the empirical bases of today's understanding of construction.

In recent years, during field studies in Egypt (Cairo) and Indonesia (Sumatra), as well as my teaching at the ETH Zurich, I have investigated how construction, ethnography and the climate can be considered together.[6] I use exhibitions to exploit the visual potential of such empirical, reflexive research.

Interdisciplinary work is part of architects' day-to-day tasks. The urgent question however is where architects see their core competence and what they feed back into their actions (in practice and research) as externalised elements of their field of knowledge by bringing in specialists. By externalising building-technical and structural-physical knowledge from construction, architecture has resigned a core competence of builders that is thousands of years old and delegated it to specialists. While it is still natural to react differentiatedly to the relevant dominant climate through the clothes we wear, an industrialised western building culture has allowed the climate to become a purely technical problem that is addressed by machines and installations.

[6] Seminar at the ETH Zurich: Einführung in die ethnografische Forschung der modernen Architektur. See: http://www.deplazes.arch.ethz.ch/dplz_site/index.php?nav=lehre&id=81 (date: 1.3.2013)

Thanks to thermodynamic knowledge of physics, we have indeed exact parameters with which to describe the climate; yet we lack in-depth knowledge on how those parameters affect structures and built forms in an architecturally significant way. Today's Architects have lost the cultural sovereignty of the field known as "building technology". The enormous challenge for contemporary architecture lies in resisting that trend, which is dictated by science, society and the building industry. The conceptual and epistemic separation of structure and building technology must be rejected by researching approaches that bring the consideration of structural thinking and building technology back together in construction.

In many places around the world today, a transformation in construction is taking place, breaking away from thousands of years of building tradition. For instance in Indonesia, a trend away from the traditional lightweight (wooden and bamboo) building methods and towards solid buildings (brick and reinforced concrete) can be observed. In Egypt, the trend is moving in a similar direction in inverse circumstances: The traditional thick-walled, solid building methods (clay and clay brick) are being replaced by lighter modern structures (brick and reinforced concrete). The climatic implications of these developments are dramatic:

The traditional buildings' climate-regulating potential is increasingly relinquished in favour of compensating air conditioning systems.
Such a general inference requires precise individual on-location studies to arrive at architecturally relevant conclusions. In 2010, during my field studies in the informal quarter of Ard el Lewa in Cairo (Egypt), I studied the continuities expressed between traditional courtyard building typologies and the contemporary informal buildings in Cairo. The typology of the informal buildings that were built on formerly fertile agricultural land reflects the former segmentation of the farmland. The principally three-sided, windowless buildings enable highly dense building aggregates, which could be extended again and again without any gaps between them.
The numerous recesses, incisions and channels that exist along the façades and inside the informal buildings serve to always provide air circulation and light to the dark interior spaces. If the channels have appropriate dimensions, they can even create a draught and thereby provide ventilation and cooling inside. From that perspective, the up to 20-storey informal high-rise buildings of today can be regarded as a further development of Arab-Egyptian courtyard buildings. These informal building types provide insight on how modernising traditional air conditioning practices can be advanced further by contemporary architects.

All images are by the author and show informal buildings in the Ard el Lewa quarter in Cairo

Simply Complex

Climate and energy in Switzerland since 1950

Christoph Wieser

As has been the case in the past, climate and energy act as two of many design factors. For instance, in Lugnez in the Grisons region, buildings did not always, as one might expect, depend on the topography and exposure of the living area: "On flat settlement areas there was no need for a topographical order and the buildings were aligned more freely, mostly however taking the living room's exposure to sunlight into account. Even at the time however (17th century), the façades of large farmhouses and mansions were aligned towards squares and streets."[1]

The described freedoms refer to an important aspect: While the inclusion of climatic factors in simple vernacular buildings was essential, the financial means of mansion builders have always allowed them to ignore at least some climatic conditions and compensate for them using technical facilities. That was easier in temperate climate zones than elsewhere; today's building materials and building technology – combined with an according energy input – can in any case compensate for almost any architectural and conceptual shortfall with respect to climate considerations.

Walter Gropius, and with him many representatives of modern architecture, foresaw an internationalisation of architecture in which the similarities would be greater than individual and national differences. In his famous publication "Internationale Architektur", Gropius justified the will "to develop a uniform world image" that characterised the period: "A uniformity of modern building that is characterised by global travel and technology, crossing natural boundaries that remain bound to nations and individuals, is breaking ground in all cultured countries."[2] As we know, the buildings in the International Style were not quite as uniform as he had imagined. Nevertheless, the rapid development of "global technology", which for instance manifested itself in building technology and happened at the same time as the spread in modern buildings, certainly supported the proclaimed uniformity.

[1] Fachhochschule beider Basel, Abteilung Architektur (Ed.): Val Lumnezia. Haus – Siedlung – Landschaft. Muttenz 2005. p. 88

[2] Gropius 1925. p. 7 [trans.]

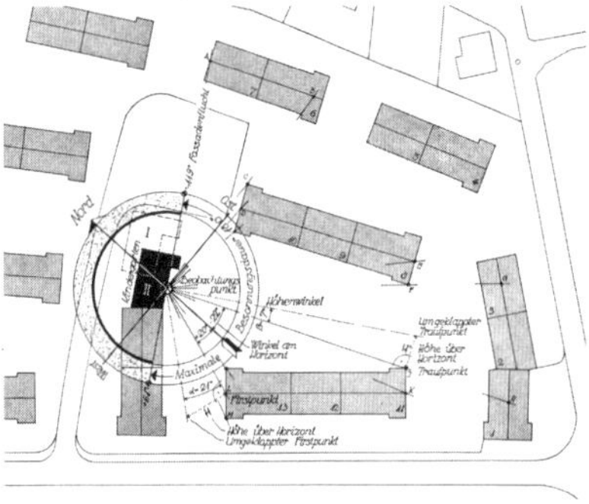

Hans and Gret Reinhard: Method to assess the sunlight exposure of a construction site with the example of the planned Stöckacker kindergarten, 1949. In: Werk, Nr. 3. Zurich 1949, p. 73

On the other hand, already in the early 1930s, in some countries – including Switzerland – a particular variation of modern architecture developed.[3] There have always been architects that particularly weighted their designs towards climate or energy aspects, seeking to study regional building traditions. Outstanding examples since the 1950s are presented below.

Modern Swiss buildings from the 1940s may appear to be rather traditional from a formal perspective, but conceptually, most of them are further developments of the rational principles of Functionalism. Hans and Gret Reinhard developed such a systematic study of climatic aspects. They published their method to assess the sunlight conditions affecting a plot in 1949.[4] Their decidedly scientific approach with an exactly calculated process can be regarded as a further development of the modernist distance or cross-sectional diagrams, into which the angle of the sunlight was inserted to calculate building distances. This type of study had a formal effect on the design of buildings only in the following decade.

In the early 1960s, the search for new forms of living that allow a condensed, single-family-home way of life led to the renaissance of the courtyard building in the form of "carpet housing estates", as well as terraced houses and stepped houses. With respect to energy and climate aspects, the stepped house appeared to be especially interesting, although it was often problematic in other respects.[5] The stepped house has long been known as a building type, as the American Pueblos and Mediterranean examples show. But it only became widespread in Europe in the 1960s and was even a popular element of Utopian urban planning.[6] Stepped houses were also planned in Switzerland: In October 1964, the magazine Werk dedicated an entire issue to it, while two years later, a second issue covered the same theme. The reasons for the boom were diverse, but the introductory text primarily stressed the economic arguments. Stepped buildings provided an "opportunity to densely develop steep slopes that had previously hardly been developed, or only with great difficulty, and were therefore (initially) cheap even when in excellent residential areas."[7] Surprisingly, the climatic advantages offered by stepped housing are not even mentioned in either of the two magazines. For instance Claude Paillard only briefly

[3] Cf. Christoph Wieser: Erweiterung des Funktionalismus 1930–1950. Mit Beispielen aus der Schweiz und Schweden (Dissertation EPF Lausanne). 2005

[4] Reinhard 1949. p. 72–74

[5] Stepped houses do not only have advantages: Building on a slope is demanding in terms of construction and supplies, and there is often the question of the compatibility of such solutions with the urban planning.

[6] Individual megastructures of this kind were built, for instance the London Brunswick Centre by Patrick Hodgkinson with Leslie Martin (1972), a platform that is delimited by two opposite rows of stepped housing.

[7] Scherer 1966. p. 201 [trans.]

[8] Paillard 1961. p. 55 [trans.]
[9] Gisel 1960. p. 126

stresses the advantages of the wind-shielded sun-trap in his comment on the stepped house in Zurich-Witikon (1960), which was published in 1961: "The rooftop terrace and garden provide a fully adequate additional living space on pleasant days, especially since they are protected from the wind and outside views by lateral slat walls running diagonally down the slope."[8] He does not discuss climatic aspects of the design any further, although he does mention a special additional aspect: The apartments are not simply stacked on top of each other, but are stepped in their cross-section; the entrance is a number of steps lower than the rooftop terrace. Paillard and Leemann use that measure to adjust to the slope, which is actually too gentle for the size of the apartments – thereby creating a spatial tension, since the movement in the apartment is actually contrary to the slope in order to stage the "climb to the roof", as Paillard expressed it. Furthermore, what is of particular interest here is that the measure allows sunlight to shine further inside the apartment than would be the case in a conventional floor design.

The terrace is also an especially important place in the holiday home by Ernst Gisel in Rigi-Kaltbad (1959) since, "in fine weather, it becomes the most used living area," as he wrote.[9] The climatic conditions of the building site define the character of Gisel's holiday home on different levels. The south-western alignment enables ideal use of the winter sun, which is supported by the building form: While the house has two storeys on the western and southern

Claude Paillard, Werner Jaray and Peter Leemann: Stepped house in Zurich, 1960. In: Werk 2–1961. p. 54/55

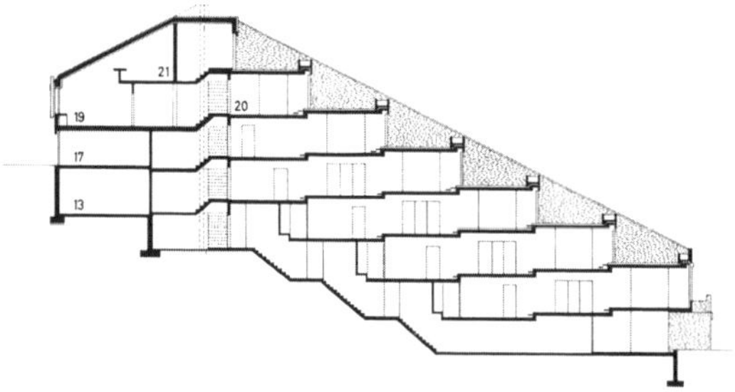

sides, the roofline falls diagonally to produce a single storey at the north-eastern corner. A central element of the interior is the two-storey area, from where the stairs lead to the gallery floor with the bedrooms, and where the cockle stove is situated: just like in old farmhouses, where the kitchen reaches under the roof to allow the smoke to dissipate and the heat radiation of the fire to be used to warm up the neighbouring rooms. Traditional concepts to optimise the heat balance were picked up and reinterpreted in this way by Ernst Gisel to create contemporary architecture that was unique in Switzerland at the time.

In late 1973, the oil crisis caused enormous shockwaves that have rightly been described as a "revolution".[10] The shortage of crude oil forced industrialized nations to completely rethink their current lifestyles and production methods, which were based on the existence of large amounts of cheap energy. This dependency was exemplarily apparent in the building industry, where the increasing demand for comfortable living developed during the economic boom was adressed by means of great energy consumption and technical investment. Suddenly, the problematic aspects of internationalisation became apparent: "One must admit that it is absurd to build the same buildings in Brasilia and Novosibirsk, in Chandigarh and Vancouver, in Sweden and Rome. The heat loss of glass boxes and the necessity to cool rooms during the summer in temperate countries like ours are serious mistakes for which we must pay the true price now."[11]

In April 1974, the magazine Werk reacted with a theme-related issue on 'urban planning and architecture in view of a painful transformation' to adapt to limited energy resources.[12] The impotence of architects at the time, as well as the great continued trust in technical solutions, is for instance apparent in that issue in the fact that it is almost exclusively written by engineers. The most important measures are listed as heat insulation for the building shell, a shift from lightweight building to an increase in the storage mass, reduced glass areas and the use of double-glazing, no air conditioning systems and the replacement of individual building heating with long distance heating. The most sensible type of heating is described as "emission, presuming there are enough emission surfaces

[10] "This winter, a deep-rooted revolution has struck developed countries – be they capitalist or dirigiste." Stierlin 1974. p. 416 [trans.]

[11] Stierlin 1974. p. 417 [trans.]

[12] Werk Nr. 4. Zurich 1974. p. 415–438

Ernst Gisel: Holiday home in Rigi-Kaltbad, 1959. In: Werner Oechslin, Bruno Maurer (Ed.), Ernst Gisel Architekt, 1993, Zurich. p. 93

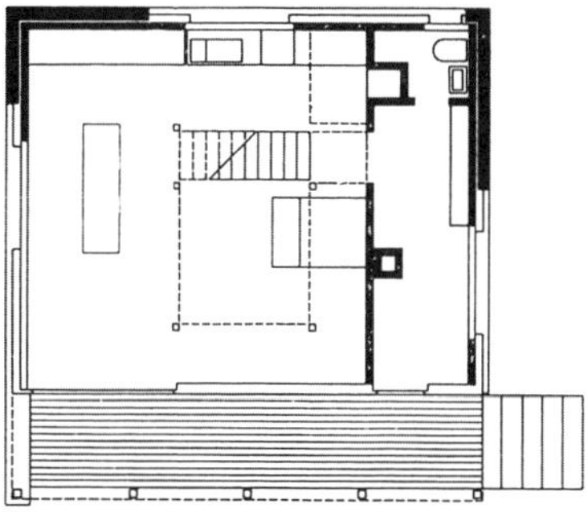

Ernst Gisel: Holiday home in Rigi-Kaltbad, ground floor, 1959. In: Werk 4–1960, p. 126

[13] Rieben 1974. p. 430
[14] Exactly two years after the "energy issue", Werk published one on the architecture of nuclear power stations. Cf. Werk Nr. 4. Zurich 1976
[15] Cf. Alder 2006
[16] Zophoniasson 2006. p. 26. As early as in 1955, G. E. Kidder Smith described the climatic aspect of the loggia and its variations and utilization in the different regions of Italy. Cf. G. [George] E. [Everard] Kidder Smith: Italy Builds. London: Architectural Press 1955. p. 34–39
[17] Alder and Vogt 1981, p. 26–27
[18] Sabady 1978. p. 18 [trans.]
[19] Sabady 1978. p. 19 [trans.]

(walls, ceilings) with a low temperature. To be effective, such a system must be operated electrically."[13] That and the strong arguments in favour of long distance heating, represented substantial economic interests: The electrical industry and the nuclear power lobby[14] sensed a great opportunity to fill the gap the oil industry had at least temporarily left behind.

And what about the architects? Apparently some were initially of the opinion that the problem could be solved technically. The slow reaction time also no doubt had to do with the recession that followed the energy crisis. One interesting exception was Michael Alder, who studied under Aldo Rossi at the ETH Zurich and then encouraged debate on typology as a Lecturer at the Technikum in Muttenz, Basel, thereby developing an individual architecture. Numerous field studies, especially on rural architecture in southern Switzerland, show his interest in elementary building forms, basic types and their variations.[15] One of his favourite themes was the loggia, to which he dedicated a seminar trip to the Val Sesia in 1990. As can be seen in the introduction to the accompanying documentation, he was very aware of the climate aspects of that building element.[16] In 1979, Michael Alder carried out an initial design study on an energy-saving house in Muttenz contracted by the Basel Building Authority.[17] A caretaker's house was planned with the aim of finding "an economic and energy-saving solution". Alder proposed a compact building volume with an integrated "sun oriel". All utility rooms are oriented towards the south, and the windows on the south side are larger than those on the north. The house is well insulated, is solidly built to make the most of the sunlight and uses a projecting south-facing pergola for cooling in the summer. The heating system consists of warm air collectors, a water tank, floor heating, a gas instantaneous water heater, a warm air fireplace and the above-mentioned sun oriel. It therefore covers all themes that were increasingly important in the late 1970s and early 1980s: using solar energy and zoning the floor plans and sections based on energy considerations.

Michael Alder: House in Liestal, 1981. In: Ulrike Zophoniasson-Baierl 2006, p. 73

Pierre Robert Sabady, who was born in Hungary and is resident in Switzerland, is regarded as a pioneer of solar energy use. From the mid-1970s onwards, he published several books on the subject and managed a specialised design office. In 1978, he published his "seven pillars of the biosolar building principle" in an issue of the magazine Werk/Archithese that was dedicated to the subject of the "position of the sun".[18] The principles are interesting since they describe important points on optimising the energy consumption of a building from an architectural perspective. Sabady also touches on technical matters, but he considers the spatial, volumetric and material disposition – i.e. the factors relevant to design – to be more decisive. In his own words, that means: optimised location, southern orientation, thermal zone planning, a compact building volume, an inclined roof, a projecting roof to protect the façades, and biophysically optimised building materials, building elements and technical systems. To illustrate those "pillars", he chose the "Biosolar House Hälg" he designed in Lucerne as an example. The ground plan has a trapezoid shape, whereby its southern side is widest and has large surfaces, while the northern side with auxiliary room has almost no windows at all. The section shows different thermal buffer zones, whereby Sabady distinguishes between interior and exterior zones. Interior zones for him include the staircase, corridors, cellar and attic; exterior zones include the conservatory, garage and games room. He is convinced that, "by systematically applying thermal buffer zones combined with heat recovery [the] heating requirements of a house [can be] reduced by 50%."[19] Furthermore he states that the slanting design of the southern façade could improve the effectiveness of the warm air collectors.

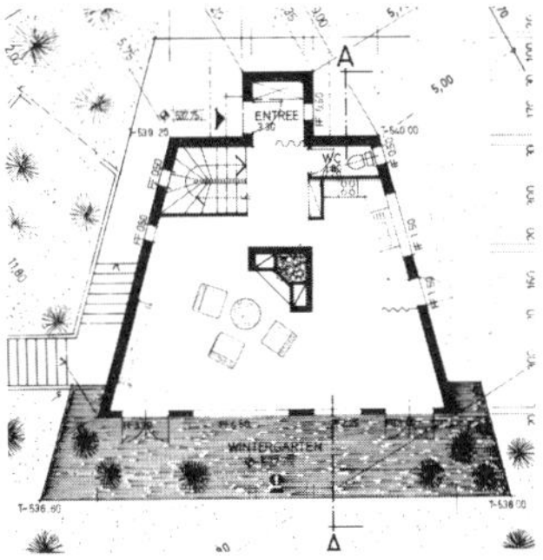

Pierre Robert Sabady: Project "Biosolarhaus" Hälg near Lucerne, 1977.
In: Werk/Archithese, 19–20 (July/August) 1978. p. 18

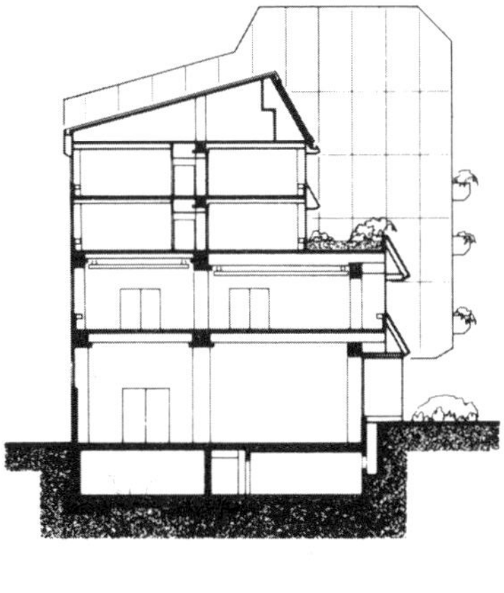

Pierre Robert Sabady with Bruno Winkler, office building of the Micafil machine works in Zurich-Altstetten, 1979. In: Schweizer Ingenieur und Architekt, Heft 45 1979. p. 907 and 909

The same principle partially characterises the Micafil Building in Zurich Altstetten, which was produced in collaboration with Bruno Winkler. The company Micafil developed, produced and sold special electrical products. Following the oil crisis, it started to "systematically address the problem of energy value analysis and the potential of eco-technology".[20] In that context the new building, which faces the south-east and was built in 1979, represents a demonstration of the company's philosophy. The building's sectional view shows it to have a staggered volume, whereby air and solar collectors occupy the diagonal balustrade bands and the slanting roof. The applied methods, such as taking the different positions of the sun in the winter and summer into account, the effect of the storage mass and the ground plan's zones have been known since ancient times. So it is no surprise that Sabady's Hälg home has similarities with a systematic representation of Socrates' "Solar House Concept", which the architect himself illustrated as a reference in his book "Haus und Sonnenkraft", which was published in 1975.[21]

The ecological movement in the 1980s picked up on the use of natural materials and energy saving potential, and developed them further. They included "exotic" approaches such as Peter Vetsch's earth and cave houses,[22] as well as more conventional solutions. Perhaps the most important attribute of energy-conscious building since the 1970s has been the conservatory or – a more extensive variation on that theme – enveloping entire buildings with thermal buffer zones. Such "pullovers" highlight the call to build in a sparing way on a symbolic level and also communicate a return to greater autonomy and less dependence on technical machinery as aspects of the aspired attitude.

In the 1990s, the significance of the architectural envelope shifted: The climatic aspect was displaced by a visual method of design and work. The success of a layered façade principle for reasons of structural physics led to the structural autonomy of the building shell, which took place on an according design level. Furthermore, technical developments in the window industry led to surprising improvements in insulation values, allowing larger window areas to be used once more. Contemporary, largely glazed buildings – such as the teachers' seminar in Chur by Bearth & Deplazes (1999) – impressively show

Peter Vetsch, house in Raven, Ascona, 1982.
In: Vetsch 1994. p. 44

[20] Micafil is now a subsidiary of ABB.
[21] Sabady 1976. p. 20
[22] Vetsch 1994

how the formulae for climate-conscious buildings established in the 1970s (closed north façade, large open areas on the south façade) no longer fully applied. The constant improvements in materials enabled solutions that appeared to be inconceivable only a short time earlier. Alongside the continous increase in the proportion of glazed surfaces, this also included the return of exterior load-bearing structures, which intersect the insulating perimeter many times – an option that had been taboo for around 20 years for reasons of construction physics.
Due to the new possibilities of engineering, the architectural study of climate aspects was again pushed into the background for some time. During that period, it seemed as if a renaissance in technical solutions for energy and climate aspects was emerging, by for instance insulating the shell in ever better ways, while architectural conception was not questioned any further. Nevertheless, the constant, striking increase in the energy balance requirements of a building in our region no longer allows such an unconsidered approach: A thick insulation layer alone is not nearly enough today. Much is also demanded from the building technology. The tendency towards as compact volumes as possible is closely linked to the necessity of fulfilling the aspired energy standards.
In the work by Herzog & de Meuron, a number of buildings exemplarily demonstrate the shift in significance of the building's envelope away from the heat buffer to a pictorial design – for instance the conversion of the SUVA Building in Basel (1993), where Herzog & de Meuron connect the existing and the extension buildings with a surrounding layer of glass. The insulating glass not only improves the energy values of the old building, but is also used architecturally to homogenise old and new elements. They also use printed glazing for the Pfaffenholz sports facility in St. Louis (1993). The multilayered façade structure and the visual finishing work on the shell are the most important design elements of the exterior. The panes of smoked glass are additionally printed – using the motif of the surface structure of the cement-embedded wood wool plates that are used as insulation a few centimetres behind the layer of glass. The thermal insulation fulfils its structural-physical purpose and at the same time becomes a template for the texture. The layer of insulation contributes to

[23] Luchsinger 1998. p. 36
[24] Wirz 2005. p. 62 [trans.]

enhancing the attractiveness of the building shell, while its symbolic value as an indicator of ecologically conscious building methods is apparently outdated.

In addition to the theme of building envelopes and covering, consideration of the building structure as a means to improve the energy balance became increasingly important in Switzerland in the mid-1990s – which entailed studying the design aspects of energy and climate factors beyond technical solutions. As already mentioned, the 1970s saw an intentional move away from lightweight building methods and towards the use of building mass for storing heat. That principle, which had hardly been systematically applied before, was picked up by Bearth & Deplazes for their school buildings in Vella (1997), developing it further to such an extent that there was no need to install any heating. This was a novelty in Switzerland.[23] The buildings are made of concrete and externally insulated. Combined with the cone-shaped windows, that creates ideal conditions for using the passive sunlight. The solar energy is stored in the stone slab flooring and the ribbed concrete ceilings. The ceilings play a central role: "By creating a ribbed profile, the distribution of mass

Herzog & de Meuron: Conversion and extension, SUVA Building in Basel, 1993. In: Gerhard Mack, Herzog & de Meuron. Das Gesamtwerk Band 2, 1996, Basel/Boston/Berlin. p. 44

and therefore the heat absorption is improved in the ceilings. To reflect a maximum amount of sunlight onto the ceiling, diverting slat blinds are essential on the inside of the windows. Depending on the position of the slats, not only the heat absorption of the ceiling is activated, but also the natural lighting is improved deep inside the rooms, which considerably reduces electricity consumption for lighting."[24] The design of the ceiling and other building units as multifunctional elements characterises the design, which uses genuine architectural means to optimise the energy balance, rather than elaborate technology.

Bearth & Deplazes, school building in Vella, 1997. In: Heinz Wirz (Ed.), Räumlinge. Valentin Bearth & Andrea Deplazes, 1999, Lucerne. p. 41

Philippe Rahm – Climate and Typology

In traditional architectural theory, we speak of "architectural elements" and "composition principles". Architectural elements usually mean individual parts such as stairs, walls, doors, supports, etc. Composition principles are formulae that use a number of individual elements to develop ground plans, for instance using addition, subtraction, symmetry, asymmetry and so on.
In view of today's interest in the climate and sustainability, we wish to shift those traditional elements from the concrete to the ethereal, from the tectonic to the climatic. We propose introducing factors such as heat, humidity, air and light as new composition principles based on climate-related phenomena. New composition principles based on meteorological factors, such as convection, heat conduction, evaporation, air pressure and heat radiation should also be adopted.
Architecture should no longer be satisfied with creating spaces, but should instead create temperatures and atmospheres.

The Example of Evaporated Rooms, Philippe Rahm architectes 2011

Example: The Example of Evaporated Rooms, 201, apartment for a young doctor. Architects: Philippe Rahm architectes with Renaud Pinet, Mathieu Bujnowskyj, Huguet Marina i Blasi. Client: Louis Malachane, Location: Perrache, Lyon, France. Total floor space: 60 m^2. Design period: 01/11–06/11, Construction period: 09/11–12/11.

To achieve the aim of energy savings in accordance with the guideline SIA 3842, the temperature should be adapted according to the activity in the room. We must therefore physically separate all rooms and functions by walls or closed doors so that the different temperatures in the individual rooms are not mixed and evened out like hot and cold water. To implement the recommendations of the SIA, one would have to do without the plan libre and the spatial continuity developed by Modernism, returning to the closed architecture of the 19th century, when every room formed an independent unit due to its walls and doors. We can begin composing rooms – i. e. distributing functions in space without needing to define contours with walls – by making use of the spatial layering of air temperatures to allocate functions. We therefore propose not to design rooms and areas, but instead to allocate usage (and therefore the location of furniture) to specific places, at specific heights, with specific temperatures and specific lighting conditions. The reading armchair, which is used alone, is given a place at the highest area of

warm air, as is the shower, where one is strongly exposed to temperature shifts. The communally used sofa has a slightly lower position, since there is more heat when several people sit together. The kitchen should be positioned even lower to be able to use the cooler room climate, and finally the bed is in the coolest part of the house, on the ground floor.

Example: Domestic Astronomy, 2009, Louisiana Museum of Modern Art, Humlebæk, Denmark. Green Architecture for the Future, Exhibition 29. 5.–4. 9. 2009. Philippe Rahm architectes. Climate software and programming in collaboration with fabric.ch. Drawings by Amy O'Neill.

"Domestic Astronomy" is the prototype of an apartment in which one now inhabits the air space rather than the area. Functions and furniture are raised from the floor, distributed around the entire height and given a location in the spatial volume that has the most suitable temperature depending on the body, clothing and activity.

Domestic Astronomy, 2009

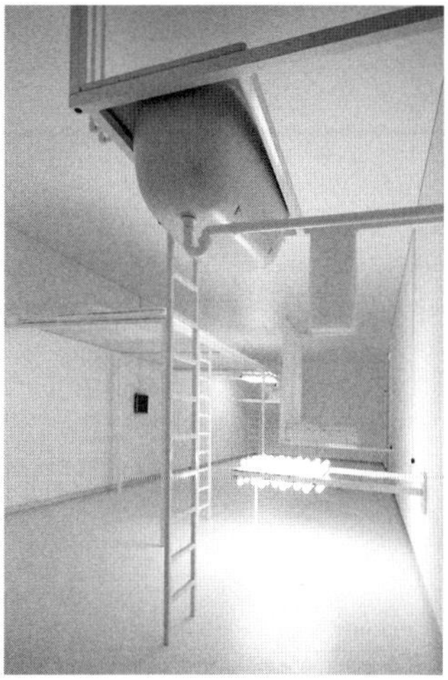

Strategy

Christian Hönger, Roman Brunner

Design is regarded as the supreme discipline in architecture. It denotes the coherent implementation of a programme in a spatial form and its integration into an urban planning situation while taking specific architectural intentions into account.[1] It is assumed that aspects of climate, resources and energy play a decisive, inspiring role in influencing the form, typology, construction and materials.[2] In terms of the climate, one can distinguish between two underlying approaches: The currently widespread "compensation method" is a "high-tech method" and is aimed at compensating climate conditions using highly developed building technology. The other approach is the so-called "empathy method"[3], a "low-tech method" aimed at reacting to the climate using form and space itself. It aims to save or actively gain as much energy as possible using as little technology as necessary. The "empathy method" is for the longer term and more autonomous with respect to political decisions and underlying economic conditions. It develops an inventive, tailored reaction to the climate and can produce a localized, specific architecture. The balance between outside and inside, between climate and comfort, is achieved through intelligent, primarily spatial and structural means that integrate physics, biology[4] and technology. The technology is thereby merged with the architecture itself and integrated into early design stages as a cultural, technical influencing factor.[5]

In this sense, the building (after clothing) is regarded as people's third skin and an organism that can react – and not as lifeless materials in which the climate-compensating machine must be installed.[6] This perspective is not only limited to architecture, but also raises the question whether a highly technological world is even worth striving for and whether we can or wish to afford it in the long term.[7] The role and function of technology can now be reinterpreted, regarded and applied mainly as an intelligent, fast method of evaluating and simulating a comprehensive and therefore ideal solution approach.[8]

[1] Hassan Fathy pointedly comments as follows: "When an engineer designs a machine, a bridge or a controller, every line he produces is the result of very many laws and principles of a wide range of engineering sciences. The technician develops the machine to comply with precisely defined specifications and to carry out specialised work. In both cases, he must draw from everything he has learnt in the fields of physics, dynamics, construction engineering and material science. The same group of engineering laws defines every line drawn by an architect designing a building or a city – however together with a whole collection of other sciences with fields that are less exactly defined: sciences that deal with people and their relationship with the environment and society. Such fields – Sociology, Economics, Climatology, Architectural Theory, Aesthetics and the study of culture in general – are just as important to architects as the other engineering sciences, because they directly deal with people, for whom the architecture exists." Fathy 1987. p. 34–49 [trans.]

[2] Konstantinidis, Aris / Rudofsky, Bernard

Let us call such planning, which is adapted to the relevant climate in the sense of a direct design activity, a "strategy of action". The strategies of action presented here highlight the fact that the underlying decisions with respect to the energy balance of a building are made early on in the design process. Depending on the climatic conditions, different spatial strategies can be selected, which are presented individually below as architectural measures. Some strategies influence the use of the building and lifestyles. Without claiming to be exhaustive, the proposed overview aims to present underlying design applications, whereby mixed forms are also presented, since the combination of strategies is shown to be effective for some climate zones. The strategies are summarised in three main groups, "saving, yield and evasion", which are each suitable for different requirements. The approaches are mostly presented using already implemented examples, whereby other motifs have also naturally contributed to the ultimately constructed form. Most examples are residential buildings, since they are true to life and easily visualized. Strategies are also presented conceptually using icons. Supplementary texts describe the local climatic conditions, the chosen example's relationship with the strategy of action and other relevant aspects of the architecture.
Towns and urban landscapes are initially not part of our studies, since their complexity increases exponentially with the already multifaceted situation. Nevertheless, there is awareness that strategies can be applied on a large scale, are partially multipliable and can be integrated into urban structures. Nor is building renovation part of our study, even though this segment plays a major role with respect to resources and energy savings, as well as possible efficiency rates.

[3] The "empathy method" is an unprejudiced approach to existing conditions and patient assumption of the local situation. In addition to empirical knowledge, it should also apply scientific insight.

[4] Würtenberger 1989

[5] Nachtigall 2003

[6] Krausse 1995. p. 23

[7] Hassan Fathy makes the following criticism: "(...) such architecture uses high-tech materials such as a reinforced concrete frame, glass curtain façade or air conditioning. But the large majority of tropical inhabitants is industrially underdeveloped and cannot afford such high-tech luxury. For the mass of people in developing countries, the conventional energy systems of industrial countries cannot be acquired at acceptable prices. Thus there is a real need to further develop traditional systems that are based on natural resources. The traditional concept must be changed to fulfil modern requirements." Fathy 1987. p. 34–49 [trans.]

[8] Von Ove Arup developed a strategy for the school in Ladakh. Hegger, Fuchs, Stark, Zeumer, 2007. p. 231

Saving process

Saving processes are suitable for cool, sub-polar and temperate climate zones. Sub-polar climate zones are characterized by long, dry winters lasting up to 8 months and short summers, without clear seasonal changes. The average annual temperatures are below 0°C and maximum temperatures in the warmest month are 6°C to 10°C. The regions generally have low precipitation and due to their low temperatures, they have low condensation and therefore low absolute air humidity. The period of sunshine and its intensity are low in this zone.
Temperate climate zones (warm, cool and cold-temperate) are situated between the subtropics and the polar circles and have pronounced seasons. The annual average temperature is around 8°C. In the summer, the temperature can rise above 30°C, while in the winter, it can fall to below freezing. The usual heating period lies between five and seven months. Daylight hours range between 8 and 16 hours. Diffuse daylight exists during the day, since there is cloud cover for more than half of the daytime.[9] There is intensive precipitation throughout the year.

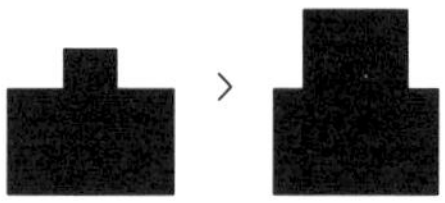

Saving 1 – Thickening

Making the volume thicker and reducing the surface area. The sheer size and proportion of a unit has a decisive influence on energy efficiency. More voluminous and deeper volumes are preferred to standard construction depths. To use them, new types of room inventions and therefore new use concepts are necessary. That need not get caught up in static approaches, since depending on the climate zone, the volume must be compact at least during the 5 to 8 winter months, yet can be exposed to sunlight in the warm season.

Example: Boba Fett, competition entry for the Werdwies estate, Bernerstrasse, Zurich, 2002, John Bosch, Andreas Kittinger, Ünal Karamuk, Jens Richter, Urs Primas. Construction engineering: Kartec, Engineering GmbH, Zollikerberg, E. Karamuk. Energy and building technology: Amstein + Walthert AG, Zurich, Hans Jürg Leibundgut. Landscape architecture: Kuhn Truninger, Zurich, Lorenz Eugster.

[9] Corrodi, Spechtenhauser 2008. p. 131

The Swiss Mittelland region, which is situated 400 to 600 metres above sea level, is in a temperate central European climate with an average annual temperature of around 10°C. The buildings in that climate zone must usually be heated for half the year. As an alternative to large main bodies with with good insulation, the thermal envelope factor[10] can be reduced. It is one of the most effective saving measures of all. That provokes typological invention since the unusual building depth strongly reduces the natural light and there are unlit spaces in the centre. As an answer, the example shows non-functional, two-storey high rooms that can be occupied and used by the residents. They are artificially ventilated, have twilight lighting conditions due to the heliostat systems and can for instance be used as media rooms.

The action mode of "thickening" was applied in several ways by the Zurich project Boba Fett: In terms of urban planning, the entire programme with 150 apartments and semi-public uses is concentrated in a single "block"[11] with 95,000 cubic metres of space and a floor area of 37 to 50 metres and a height of 51 metres.

[10] "A small thermal envevelope factor is extremely effective with respect to energy saving. An example is a semi-detached home built in 2007 with an energy reference area of 150 m² and the "Minergie-P" Standard with respect to consumption that is almost identical with a 40-unit apartment building with an energy reference area of 4,500 m² and the minimum required SIA380/1 limits." Faktor 2007. Nr. 2, 2007. p. 32 [trans.]

[11] Bosch, Kittinger, Karamuk, Richter, Prima 2002. p. 4

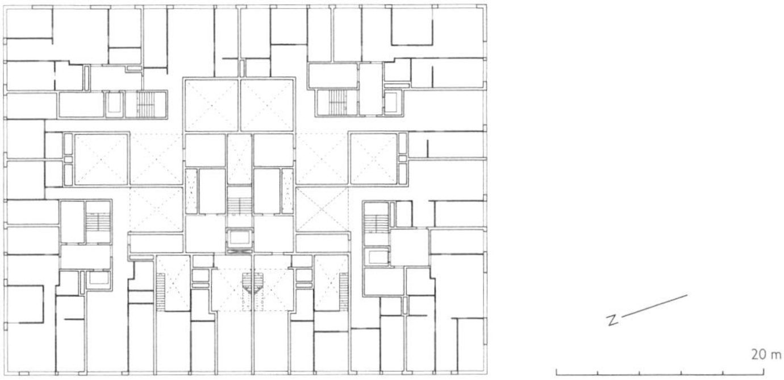

Saving 2 – Shrinking

The contracted form. Winter home; complementary to Yield 2. While in summer the entire floor space is available, the residents withdraw to a few inhabited rooms in the winter. Rooms with low comfort requirements, which need no light or air, serve as a spatial buffer with an intermediate climate. In today's buildings, the insulating perimeter can be placed around the few rooms used in the winter months or split up into several insulating layers or layered in temperature zones.

Example: Residential building combined with a stable barn, Hofstatt Zehnderhütte in Altishofen-Dorf, Lucerne, around 1650; vernacular architecture.[12]

The Wigger Valley is situated northwest of Lucerne in the transition between the Mittelland region and the Swiss Prealps. It is characterised by roughly eight months of cool to cold weather, in which temperatures can temporarily fall below –10° C, as well as high average annual precipitation levels.
The reaction to the climate is a powerful roof as protection from the rain above the multifunctional use unit for farming life with a threshing floor, livestock stables and a barn floor. To make life bearable in the transition periods and the winter, the daytime living areas are especially organised at the centre of the Hofstatt Zehnderhütte around encore heating source. Two stoves are situated in the kitchen. The tile stove for the "parlour" and the "backroom" is

[12] Brunner 1977. p. 178–191

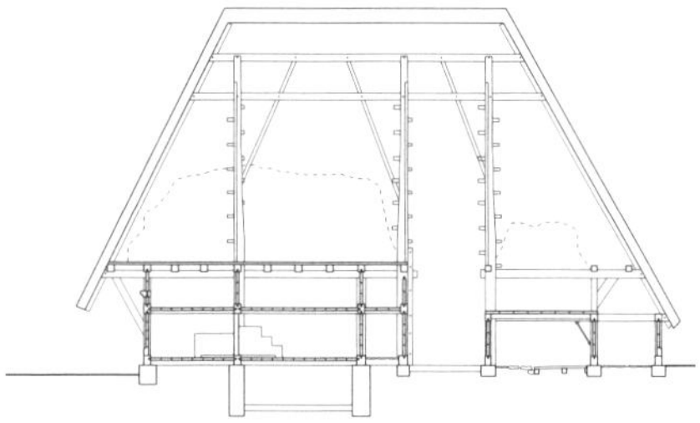

Zehnderhütte, sectional view

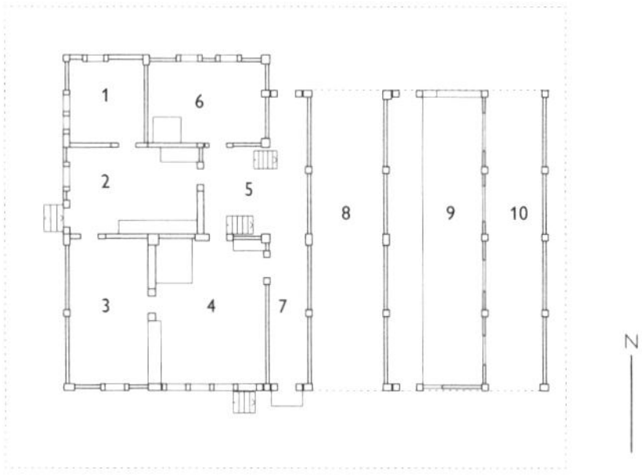

Zehnderhütte, ground floor

1 Pantry
2 Kitchen
3 Bedroom
4 Parlour
5 Forecourt
6 Back room
7 Corridor
8 Threshing floor
9 Livestock
10 Barn floor

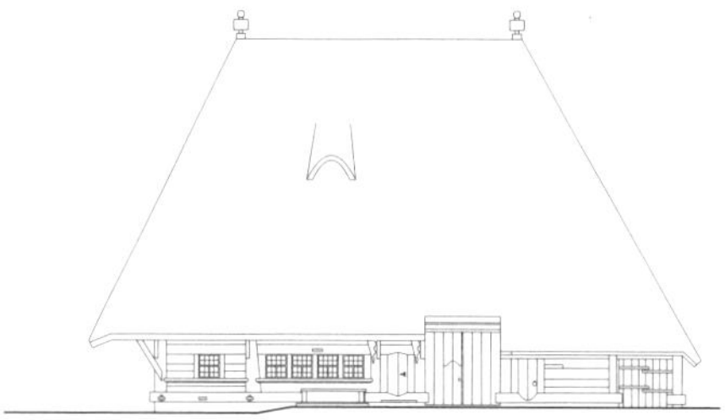

Zehnderhütte, elevation

directly connected and can be fired from the kitchen. The "parlour" and the "back room" are protected from rising damp by positioning the cellar for food beneath them. Above the kitchen, barrel-shaped smoke receptacles can be used to smoke meat, while the smoke rises between the vaults and into the vaults for the soot board on the upper floor, where it can escape via an opening on the western gable wall. To heat the bedrooms, they are only separated from the warm rooms beneath them by thin ceilings. Above the residential area is the sheaf loft, while the hayloft is above the stables. Both are filled in winter and represent a considerable insulation layer. As the warmer spring arrives, that layer gradually shrinks as it is consumed as fodder.

Saving 3 – Embedding

Digging into the terrain and covering with earth.

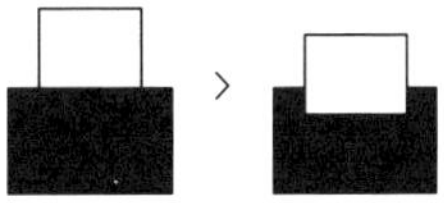

The building is submerged into the ground or largely covered. The building's mass is thereby increased and an extremely insulated, inert room climate is created that reduces the loss of energy between the building and the environment. Depending on the situation, the excavated material need not be removed and can instead be reused on location as a covering material, which is sustainable with respect to embodied energy.

Example: Turner Residence, Aspen/Colorado, USA, 1982, John Lautner (1911–1994).[13]

[13] Cohen, Olsberg, Escher 2008. p. 216–225

Aspen is situated at a high altitude of 2,400 metres in the Rocky Mountains in the State of Colorado. Colorado has a continental highland climate. The humidity is very low and the temperatures vary strongly between a maximum of 45°C to 28°C in the summer and –15°C in the winter. 700 cm of snow fall during the year.

John Lautner: Turner House, Aspen, Colorado, 1982. In: Cohen, Escher, Olsberg 2008. p. 222

The building implements the climatic conditions in two ways. A large roof covers the living space. It has the shape of a vessel and is filled with earth. The form of the roof was inspired by the shape of an oyster and approaches a semi-orb, the most efficient form of saving. The flattened shape prevents snow from sliding off it, so that large amounts of snow act as additional seasonal insulation. Almost half of the surfaces of the infrastructure rooms and one bedroom are submerged in the earth and use its compensating climate. The space-continuum in the ground plan allows all rooms to benefit from the earth's warmth and solar gains.
In addition to the saving processes, the building also achieves yields: The roof projects on all sides around the interior and is curved upwards towards the south, going against the incline of the slope, but it is shortened there to allow solar yields from large-scale glazing. A large central skylight at the gravitation point of the triangle provides warmth and light to the interior and stairs.

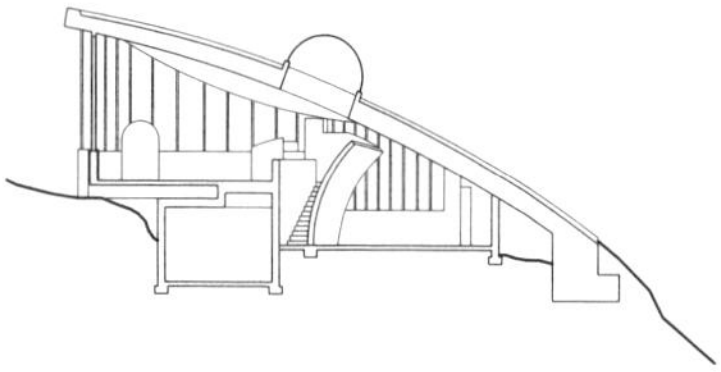

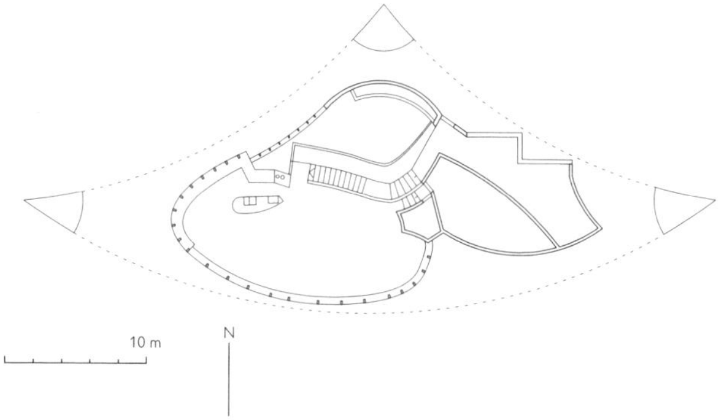

Yield process

Yield processes are suitable for temperate and mainly heat-saturated sub-tropical climate zones. Sub-tropics have a high summer and moderate winter temperature, thereby achieving the absolute highest energy radiance. The average annual temperature is above 20°C, but the average temperature of the coldest month is lower. The differences between day and night are high. The rainfall volumes in the individual zones (dry, winter humidity, summer humidity and permanent humidity) vary greatly.

Yield 1 – Exposure

The sun-shaped form

The unit's shell surfaces are aligned exactly towards the local sunshine, if necessary even bent and folded to capture as much sun as possible, both passively and actively,[14] whereby convex forms are efficient (longer exposure periods). The surfaces in the sun are more expansive, with smooth transitions from the roof to walls. By systematically taking these factors into account, the object gains an unmistakable form and is thereby localized in the landscape rather than the estate. This process mainly applies to rural regions, where the sunshine is not impeded by neighbouring buildings and thereby remains unchanged for a long time.

Example: School in Ladakh, India, 2001, Arup Associates London (design, supporting structure planning and energy concept).[15]

Ladakh is situated in the continental highland desert of the Tibetan highlands at an altitude of 3,500 m above sea level. The Tibetan highlands have very extreme climate conditions, with hot, windy summers and temperatures of up to 35°C. In the winter, (December to February), temperatures drop as low as –35°C. At night it gets cold even in the summer. At this location, the sun is the only source of energy; its yield is only required after a delay towards the evening and in the morning, so it must be stored.

The side wings of the school are aligned to provide wind protection and act as a sun trap. The quadrangular school area consists

Arup Associates: School, Ladakh, India 2001. In: Hegger, Fuchs, Stark, Zeumer, 2007. p. 231

[14] "Active" technical measures are for instance solar panels, while "passive" measures include direct solar heat gains through the windows.

[15] Hegger, Fuchs, Stark, Zeumer 2007. p. 231–233

of east-west aligned walkways with classrooms, kindergartens and crèches. The walkways have a continuous glass front towards the south, while the north side is a massive, closed wall. In the kindergarten below, an inserted skylight provides light and ventilation. The boarding school section has continuous thermopane glazing (also towards the south), which is placed in front of interior storage walls that are painted black. Towards the north, the architects reacted with an interior corridor layer as an intermediate climate in front of the massive northern stone walls. The washing and toilet facilities are concentrated and create a Trombe wall[16] orientated precisely towards the south. This Trombe wall has exterior cladding made of black painted sheet steel. Behind it is a ventilation shaft that towers above the building, with an inner clay wall that heats the interior rooms by using the phase shift.

The design typologically refers to local village and monastery structures, with its central congregation square. Planning with simulation

[16] "Félix Trombe, a French engineer, developed a massive storage wall that is dark on the outside to reflect as little sunlight as possible. In front of that wall, a glass or plastic layer is installed to convert the sun's energy into heating energy and stabilise the construction from a climate perspective. The wall is heated by the sun during the day and stores the heat energy. In the evening, it transfers the heat to the interior space." www.energieroute.de/bauen/trombe.php, 3 January 2009

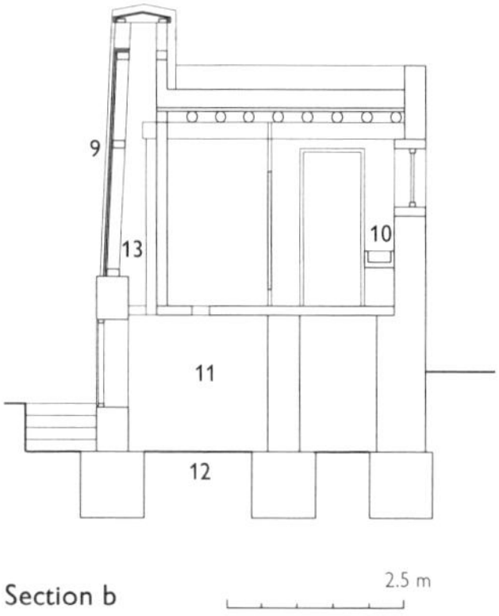

Section b

1 Entrance
2 Classroom
3 Playground with fountain
4 Crèche
5 Kindergarten
6 Classroom
7 Teacher's room
8 Wash rooms and toilets
9 Galvanised steel plates, painted dark
10 Sluice
11 Dry ditch
12 Soakaway area
13 Ventilation shaft

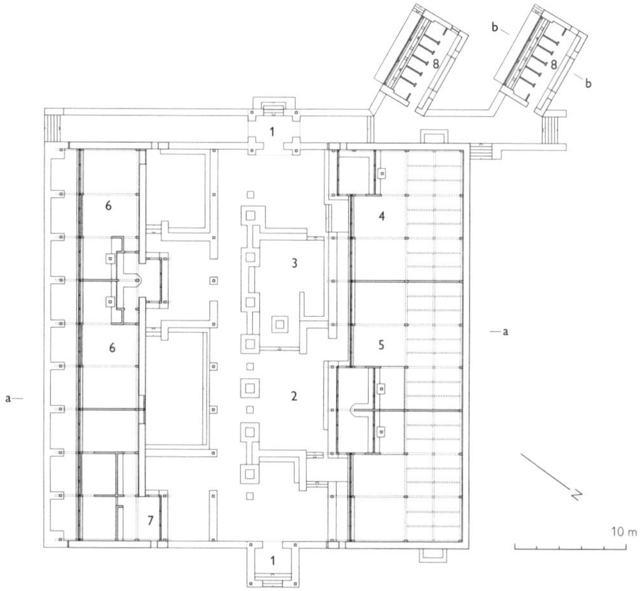

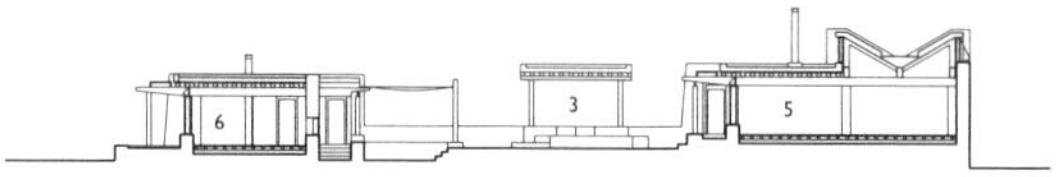

Section a

(high-tech) is combined on a high level with traditional low-tech building methods, which are integrated into the environment through the use of local materials. The natural stone walls are clad on the inside with an independent, earthquake-secure structure for the roof and walls consisting of clay tile walls and willow and poplar wood filling. The simple, traditional building method can be carried out and maintained by local day-labourers.

Yield 2 – Expansion

The summerhouse

Normally the exterior shell of a building serves as a clear climatic boundary between the inside and outside. In this strategy, the house expands in the summer, whereby a room is heated by the sun with an intermediate climate during the transition period. In the summer, the excess heat can escape through intelligently placed, natural ventilation elements.

Complementary to Saving 2.

Example: Casa Latapie Floirac near Bordeaux, 1993, Lacaton & Vassal.

Lacaton, Vassal: Casa Latapie, view from the west, Floirac, 1993. In: werk, bauen + wohnen, 1998. p. 28

Lacaton Vassal: Casa Latapie, view from the east, Floirac, 1993. In: 2G Libros Books, 2002, Barcelona. p. 26–31

Bordeaux is situated at the southern edge of a temperate climate zone. The very mild winters and the long, warm summers show the influence of the sub-tropical Mediterranean. The average annual temperature is around 13°C with an average minimum of 6°C in January and a maximum of 20°C in July. The region has high sunlight exposure, more than most other French regions (with the exception of the Mediterranean region and a few coastal regions on the Atlantic) with around 2,000 sunshine hours a year. The location has a relatively large amount of precipitation in the cooler six months of the year.

The design takes into account climate data with long transitional periods, low temperatures between early November and late February and the many sunshine hours in the year. The architects reacted to those climatic conditions with a building in two sections: a small house with a floor plan of 60 m² with an equally large conservatory

[17] Wassmer, Fischer, Zbinden 2006
[18] Flexible usability is described by Ilka and Andreas Ruby: Lacaton & Vassal. 2G Libros Books. Barcelona: Gustavo Gili (Ed.) 2002. p. 26–31

in front of it. During the transitional periods and in the summer, the house can be expanded to include the conservatory, which is heated in the morning by the eastern sun. Large foldable façade elements can be used in diverse ways to provide light, transparency, intimacy, protection and ventilation[17] and allow natural ventilation in the summer.[18]
Its two floors have a floor plan of 180 m², and cost only 110,000 CHF. It is also ecological due to its minimal material consumption and weight. To remain consistent, an existing enclosure on the street side with a natural stone base, concrete pylons and wrought iron grating was retained and integrated.

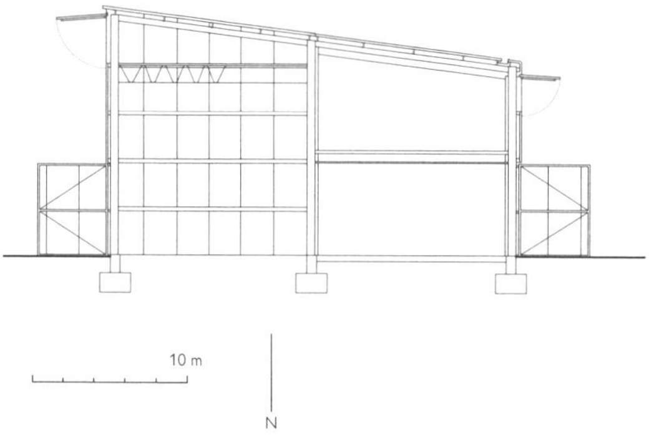

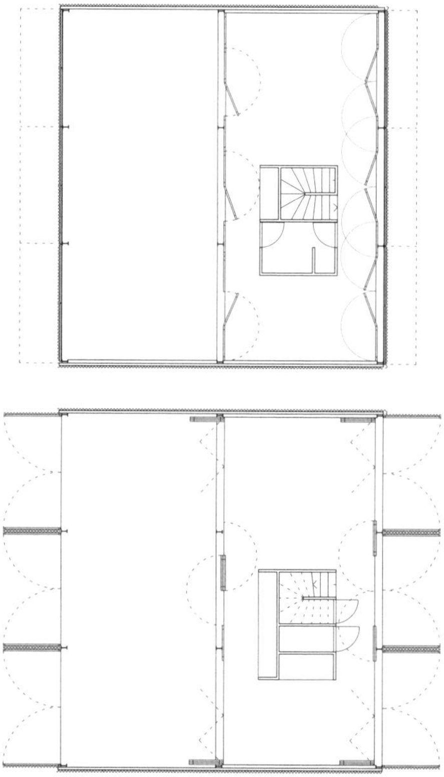

Lacaton, Vassal: Casa Latapie, ground plan and sectional view, Floirac, 1993. Aus: 2G Libros Books, 2002, Barcelona. p. 26–31

Yield 3 – Encasement

Shell with inner space, poché[19]

The outer encasement layer or the window openings enclose spaces and become voluminous sun traps towards the south and buffer zones to the north. The large southern loggia must have a cross-section that allows sunlight to shine deep into the room. In the summer, the loggia can become an open balcony to prevent overheating. Towards the north, the buffer zones can have small glass areas for auxiliary accessing use. Both voluminous shells can be designed as unheated intermediate climates.

Example: "The Growing House", Berlin 1932, Martin Wagner (1885–1957).[20]

Berlin is located in a temperate climate zone. The temperatures are balanced, in July/August around 18° C and in January/February around 0° C. The average annual temperature of 9° C is low and requires a heating period of seven months a year. The building implements the climatic conditions with a clear orientation towards the relevant directions and an onion-like spatial concept. The most intensively used and heated living room in the centre of the house is surrounded by a layer of secondary rooms. These are themselves enveloped by a spatial layer of utility rooms towards the north and a three-sided "glazed protection zone" to provide a "protective heating cover". The conservatory is explicitly not covered like "a greenhouse, but is intended as wind and sound protection". To bring as much sunlight into the room as possible, the glazed exterior walls lean towards the south, east and west.[21]

[19] The term "poché" was used in the École des Beaux Arts, but is hardly found in specialist architectural dictionaries. Poché means a form that is enveloped by a non-identical other form and is therefore mainly regarded with respect to the applied spatial and design strategy. The term is explained by Rowe Koetter 1984, p. 74–122. The phenomenon itself is also described by Venturi 1978, p. 105–136.

[20] Wagner 1932. p. 144–149

[21] The property is an element of a larger settlement with an axial structure.

Martin Wagner: The growing house, south-eastern view, Berlin, 1932. In: Wagner 1932. p. 149

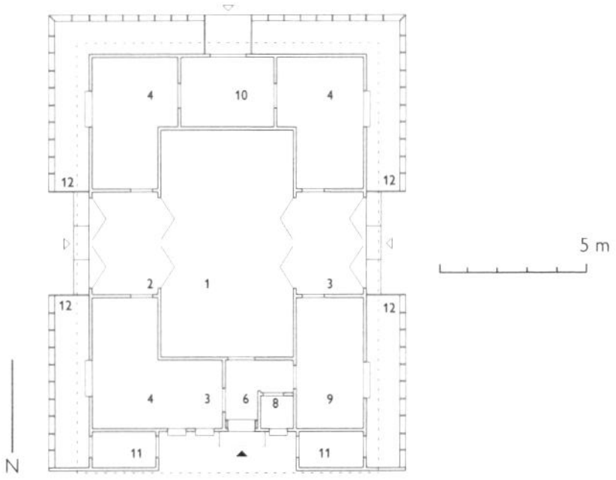

1 Living room	5 Kitchen	9 Rentable room
2 Dining area	6 Hall	10 Bathroom
3 Working area	7 Cloakroom	11 Utilities
4 Bedroom	8 WC	12 Glass-protected area

Evasion Process

Evasion processes are suitable for sub-tropical or tropical climates.

The process is especially effective in the case of extremely hot daytime temperatures or large temperature differences between day and night. The tropics (always humid, semi-humid and dry) are situated on both sides of the equator and are characterised by higher temperature shifts during the day and lower seasonal divergence (annual average of 25°C). The high level of sunlight throughout the year and the low seasonal variation, namely between 10.5 and 13.5 hours a day, mean that no thermal seasons occur.

Evasion 1 – Enclosure

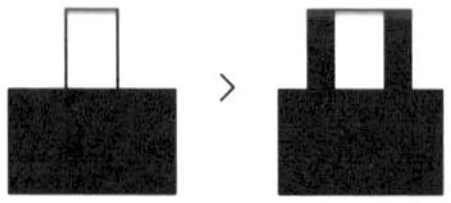

Spacious shell, "Poché"

The actual usable rooms are "captured" in the inner part of the volume.[22] The outer layer functions as structural sun protection, which keeps the sun away in the summer and allows it to enter in the winter. As a walkable balcony or a "bris soleil",[23] its depth and properties alter according to its alignment. The outermost layer determines the expression of the building.

Example: Kiritlia House, Cairo, Egypt

The City of Cairo is situated in a sub-tropical climate zone and is very hot and dry. The average annual temperature is 22°C, whereby July is the hottest month with an average of 35°C. January is the coolest month with an average of 15°C. There is very little precipitation.

To provide protection from the sun, the two inner courtyards are interwoven with cooling wells, loggias and living rooms.[24] To allow air to flow through at the same time, most of them are designed with two storeys. They are enveloped by voluminous exterior and interior walls that serve as passages or air channels, or by clay walls that act as cooled wall layers and shallow shelves for objects.

Due to their size and position, the rooms often project outwards,

[22] von Vegesack, Kries 2007. p. 110–117

[23] The bris soleil was already used in vernacular architecture, while in Modernism it was above all Le Corbusier who introduced it, implementing it for the first time in 1936 with his Education Ministry building in Rio de Janeiro. It consists of horizontal, fixed ribs in front of the façade, which prevent the rays of the summer sun to fall at a steep angle into the interior. In winter however, the sun's position is lower, allowing it to shine deep into the building. This provides solar gains and also creates a new, sculptural façade appearance.

[24] This type of interleaving could be interpreted as a forerunner of the idea of a spatial plan. By organising the room at different heights within the cubic mantle volume, there are no clear storeys. The different autonomous, mainly semi-public spatial boxes are connected to each other via openings, resulting in inner façades with diverse perspectives and complex relationships. The different levels are connected to produce a spatial continuum via inner walkways from semi-public to private areas.

towards sunlit or shady façades, constantly allowing thermal dynamics to induce moving air into the rooms. These rooms have many openings that are protected from the sun by wooden grids (known as mashrabiyas), as well as providing privacy while allowing unobserved views outside into the city. The wooden arbour on the roof also uses a finely meshed wooden structure as protection from the sun to create an intimate location. The house is an indivisible symbiosis of architecture, lifestyle, culture and climate.

Kiritlia House. In: Daidalos, 46 December 15, 1992, Berlin, p. 137

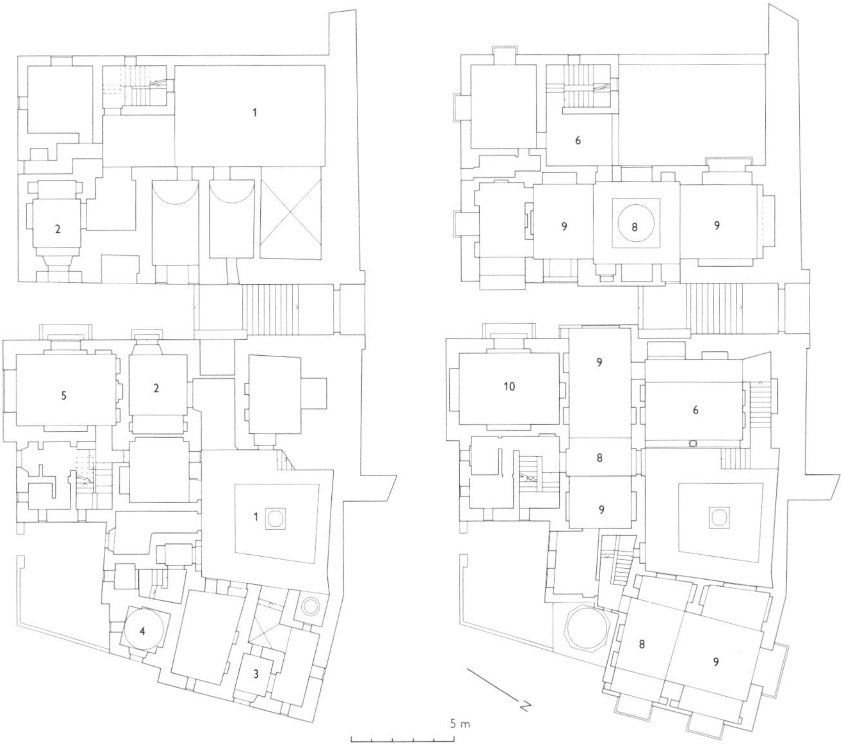

1 Inner courtyard
2 Entrance
3 Second Entrance
4 Mausoleum
5 Sabil
6 Maq'ad
7 Iwan
8 Durqa'a
9 Iwan
10 Sabil void

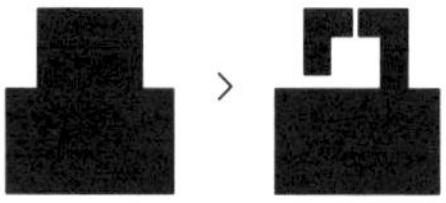

Evasion 2 – Ventilation

Cross ventilation using volume depth

Predominant winds and wind directions are used for ventilation to support the natural cooling of the building. Special facilities such as openings or towers are positioned in the direction of the cooling wind. The building is partially elevated from the ground to allow its underside to be ventilated by the wind. Open, voluminous, specifically formed roofs allow winds to pass through and transport warm air away. In additional measures, openings are placed at different heights to allow air to circulate even without wind. Such architectural elements define the building's typology and give the building its expression. Courtyards also serve to ventilate buildings in various climate zones. Often the winds pass over water areas inserted in the courtyard, which additionally cool them.

Example: Semiramis housing block, Habitations Collectives Casablanca, Morocco, 1953, Candilis Josic: Georges Candilis (1913–1995), Alexis Josic (1921–2011).[25]

[25] Joedicke 1968. p. 24–29, p. 73–75, p. 161

Candilis Josic: Habitations Collectives, Semiramis residential block, Casablanca, 1953. In: Joedicke 1968. p. 26

Casablanca has a Mediterranean climate with strong sunshine and an average annual temperature of 18°C. In August, average temperatures are the warmest at 23°C, while January is the coolest month with an average of 13°C. Average annual precipitation levels are low.

The concept of the Semiramis building is based on its cross-section: The rooms are protected from the sun by arbour passages and are also ventilated by the uncovered terraces. The individual apartments are adapted, stacked houses with an east-west alignment and daylight from two sides. The centre of the apartment is a two-storey inner courtyard that is only enclosed towards the arbour passage by a single storey, thereby constantly ventilating it. Access is provided by open stairs and arbour passages with high balustrades to ensure privacy and sun protection.

Candilis Josic: Habitations Collectives, Semiramis residential block, Casablanca, 1953. In: Joedicke 1968. p. 161

1 Entrance walkway
2 Inner courtyard
3 Kitchen
4 Shower/WC
5 Room
6 Gathering area
7 Ventilation

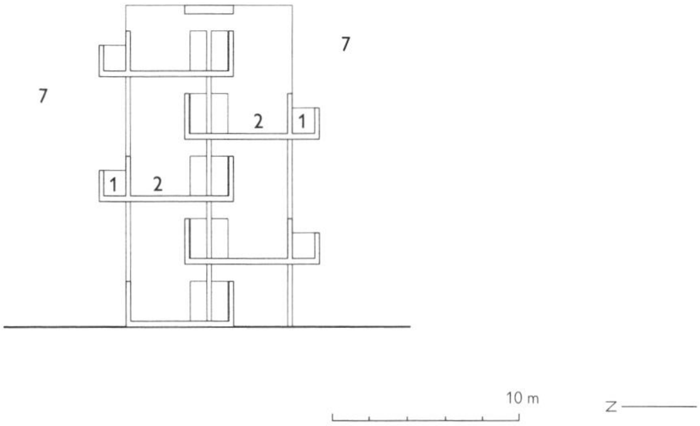

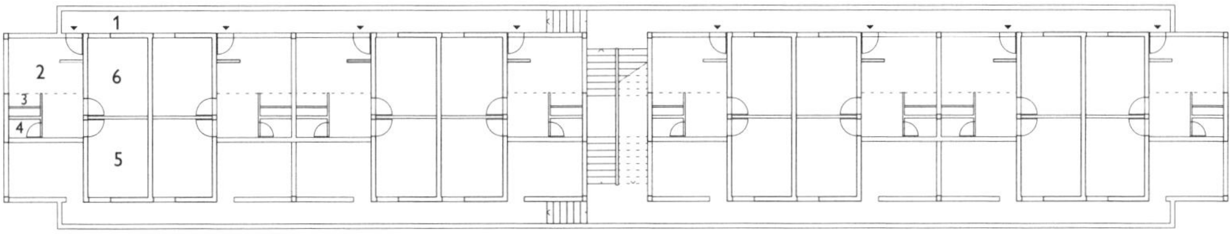

Evasion 3 – Migration

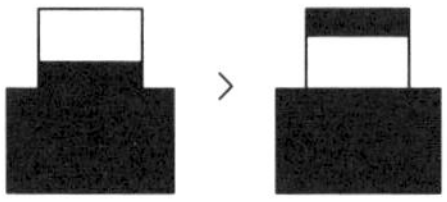

Usage-neutral rooms

The inhabited rooms alternate within the house between day and night and summer and winter. For instance the terrace is used in the summer by night and in the winter by day, while the inner space of the building is used in the summer by day and in the winter by night. To change their position without impeding their function, the various rooms must have enough area and be usage-neutral.

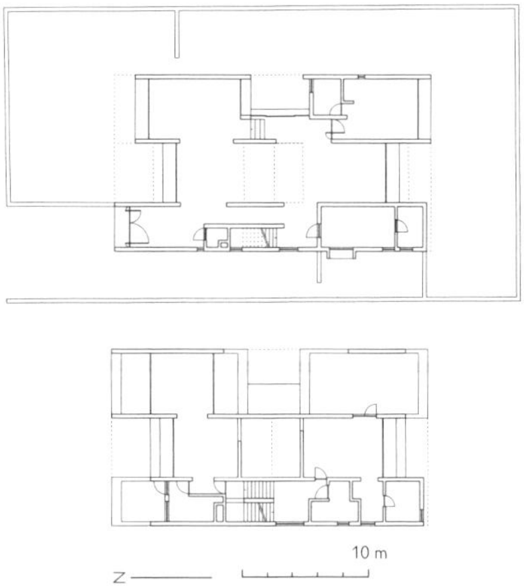

Example: Parekh House, Ahmedabad, India, 1968, Charles Correa (*1930).

Ahmedabad in western India is the city with the hottest climate in the world and is very dry: Average annual temperatures are 28°C. The months November to January are relatively cool with daytime temperatures below 30°C and nighttime temperatures around 10°C. A large proportion of the average annual precipitation falls during the monsoon season in June and July.

Charles Correa: Parekh House, Ahmedabad, India, 1968, in: Hassan-Udin 1987. p. 43

The predominantly hot temperatures make ventilated shade essential for living areas. Therefore at least half of the quadrangular mantle volume of the building is filled with air, which flows around the actual building. The roof has closely laid concrete slabs to create a horizontal bris soleil. The house is aligned exactly in a north-south direction, structured in three room layers and also has a stepped height in the north-south direction. To the west, there is an accessing and service shaft. In the centre between the service and winter areas (and therefore protected from heating), the summer area with a pyramid-shaped interior room figure and a roof with a skylight allow only little direct sunlight to enter and provide ventilation. The winter area has an inverse pyramid courtyard figure. On its roof, the bris soleil creates protected terraces with filtered light. In the north and south façades, deep concrete slabs form balustrades and lintels that act as additional sun protection.

Charles Correa: Parekh House, Ahmedabad, India, 1968, in: Hassan-Udin 1987. p. 43

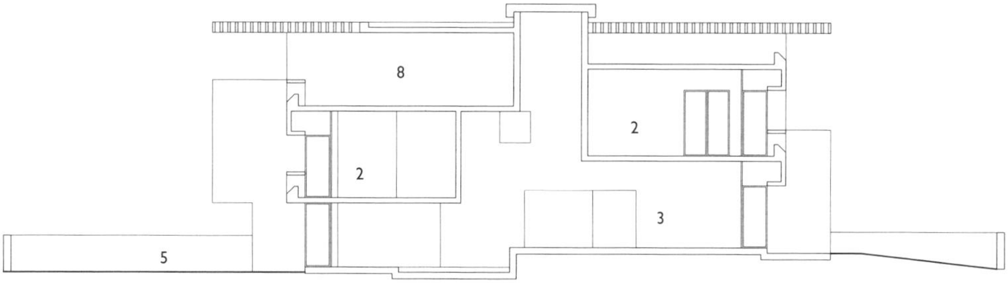

Summer house

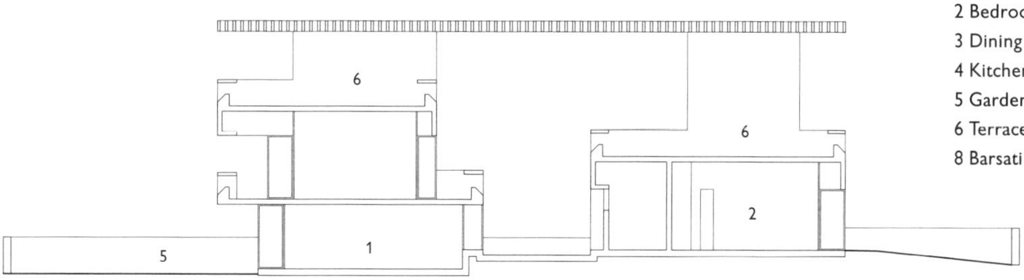

Winter house

1 Living room
2 Bedroom
3 Dining room
4 Kitchen
5 Garden
6 Terrace
8 Barsati

Mixed Strategies

Mixed strategies are combinations of saving, yield and/or evasion processes. In our temperate climate zone, a combination of saving and yield processes (and in mid-summer also evasion processes) is promising, since in winter energy is saved and solar energy yields can be generated. Flexibly planned, simple elements, such as insulated window shutters, flexible sun protection or greening, which can react well to weather, temperature and seasonal changes, are better than static measures.

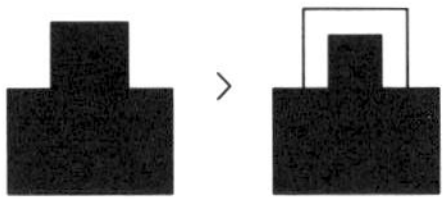

Example 1: Solar House, variable locations, Germany, 1979, Oswald M. Ungers.[26] Mixed strategy combining Saving 2 (shrinking) and Yield 3 (encasing)

[26] Ungers 1985

Germany is in a temperate climate zone with strongly varying temperatures between winter and summer. More than half the year, the buildings are heated. Since the level of annual sunshine is low, the combination of saving and yield is successful.

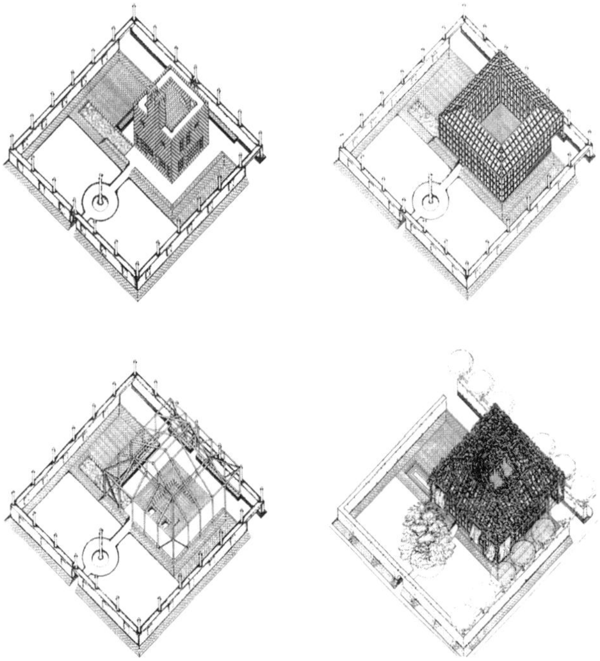

A single family home neither stands at a concrete location nor does the house have any alignment. It is called a Solar House and unifies saving and yield processes by adding different layers like an onion. A cave-like room is at the centre of the house and acts as a massive store. A solid stove heats it. A layer of infrastructure such as sanitary rooms and the kitchen to act as a three-dimensional insulation envelopes the centre. The second floor contains the individual rooms, which are also enveloped by a voluminous zone. Together they

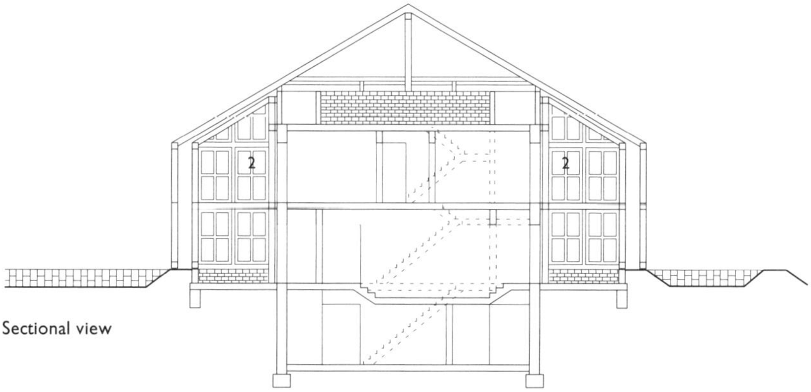

Sectional view

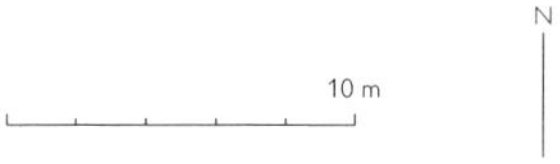

1 Veranda
2 Summer rooms
3 Garage

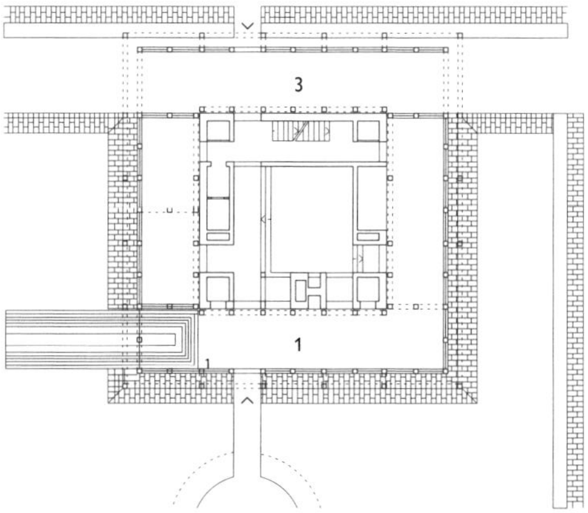

Ground floor

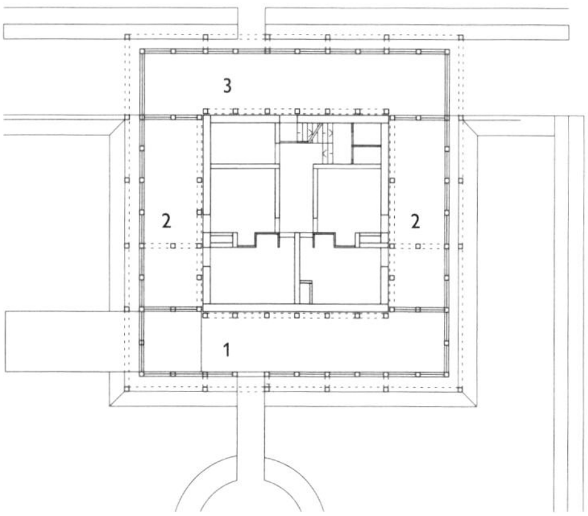

Upper floor

form the interior stone house, which is surrounded by a glass structure or a continuous veranda as a climatic buffer zone. The roof of the stone house remains open and becomes a terrace for the entire house. A pergola, which could also be described as a greenhouse since it either has latticework or is overgrown with climbing plants, forms the third layer. The green covering provides sun protection in the summer and allows light to shine inside the building during the winter, when there are no leaves. The symmetrical building is also surrounded by a symmetrical, plot-sized wall enclosure or hedge.
The matryoshka principle stacks individual archetypes of architecture – the stone house, the glass house, the greenhouse, the natural house – to create an overall building. Their interaction creates distinct interior room climates and comfortable atmospheres.

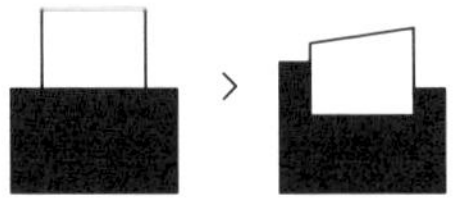

Example 2: Solar Hemicycle, Jacobs House, Middleton/Wisconsin, USA, 1944, Frank Lloyd Wright (1867–1959). Mixed strategy of Saving 3 (embedding) and Yield 1 (exposure)

Wisconsin has a continental climate that is milder due to large lakes. The summer can become hot and the winter is generally very cold. Middleton is situated near Lake Mendota, west of Milwaukee, where the average January temperature is -7 °C and the average July temperature is 21°C. The architect reacts to the cold, windy climate with two simultaneous strategies, "embedding" and "exposure". To provide wind protection, a maximum surface and minimum circumference and surface is sought for the circular overall property including the garden and house. Plants and the house itself form a protective ring around the garden. Towards the north, the house presents itself as a curved, almost closed natural stone wall, which dips into the raised ground. The largest part of the building surface is therefore buried, whereby the heat loss is reduced and the building is no longer exposed to the wind. The curved inner side of the building is oriented towards the south and acts as a passive collector with its full-surface glazing. The projecting roof keeps the summer sun out and absorbs the winter sun. All rooms can benefit from the solar gains, since the sleeping gallery is suspended into the single-room house.

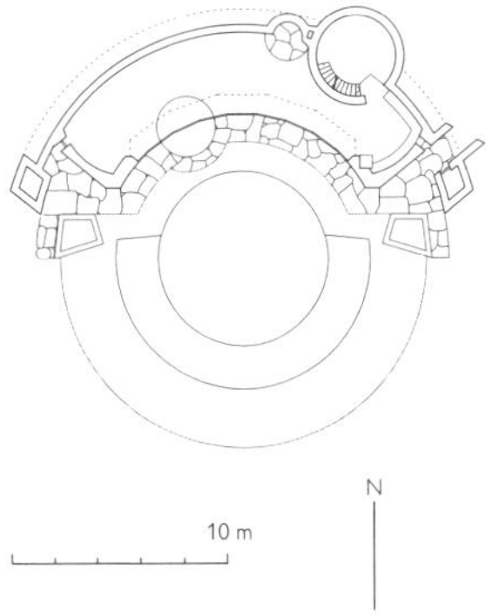

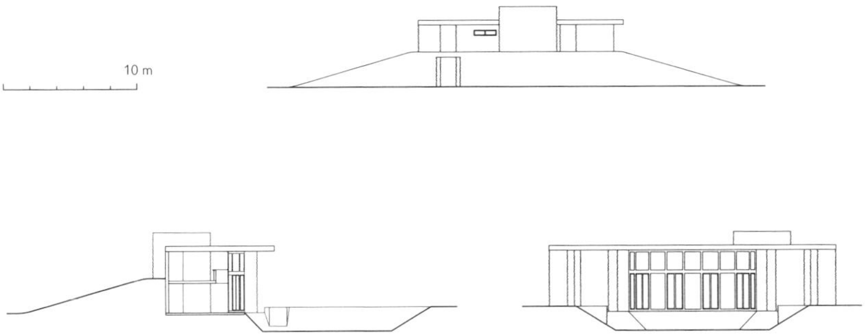

Roger Boltshauser – Climate and Material

Haus Rauch (photo: Beat Bühler)

The residential building we built known as Haus Rauch basically supports the thesis of this book. Haus Rauch is very directly characterised by the location's underlying conditions due to the locally extracted materials. 85% of the building material was directly drawn from the excavation pit. In fact it was the source of 100% of the clay walls. That also applies to the material for the sun-dried bricks that were used to externally protect the beaten cobwork walls. The other materials come from the local region whenever possible. The building therefore required around 40% less embodied energy than a building with conventional materials.

The design of the house is strongly characterised by the load-bearing qualities of the unreinforced clay walls, which can only be subjected to compressing loads. That has a considerable influence especially on the design of the apertures and the ceiling spans. The locally cut dowel ceilings, which can only be used for spans of up to five metres, as well as the fact that clay walls should take no static moment wherever possible, also had to be taken into account in the design. These design factors were all derived from the specific local material.

However not only the form, but also the resulting room conditions are dictated by the use of clay. By completely refraining from plastics, silicon and similar materials, the level of pollutant substances in the room's air is virtually zero. Another quality of the clay is the very low equilibrium moisture of 6–7%, which makes masonry mould virtually impossible. That is supported by the antiseptic effect of the clay. Odours that have a negative effect on the room air are also largely eliminated by the same clay property. With respect to thermal comfort, clay building is also advantageous compared to standard materials, as simulations have shown that the material's good hygroscopic qualities can maintain the room humidity at pleasant levels even in the summer months without additional measures. Those results suggest that buildings with air conditioning or ventilation whose spatially formative walls are aditionally plastered with clay need not be humidified. It was also surprising to discover that in operation, clay has much better thermal properties than had been assumed in advance on the basis of calculations. The difference can only be explained through new assessment of ecological building materials such as clay plaster in the master databases on which energy performance certificates are based. The named values were calculated linearly (statically), but that type of calculation does not do justice to the material properties of rammed clay. The exact energy requirement values must therefore be calculated on the basis of long-term measurements and have not yet been established. Studies have shown that there is still a need for research with respect to the core values of different types and thicknesses of beaten clay cobwork walls.

In Haus Rauch, 100% of the energy required for heating and warm water is derived from renewable energy sources. A buffer storage system is primarily supplied by the roof collectors and secondarily by the storage stove with a cooking unit in the kitchen. In the cellar, there is also a pellet heating system that heats the buffer storage system if the two other energy sources do not provide enough energy. The buffer storage provides the wall heating with the required heat. The building deliberately has no controlled ventilation or cooling system, as ventilation is achieved through circulation. The architecture is strongly characterised by the local conditions and Martin Rauch's thirty years' experience in clay building.

In addition to Haus Rauch[1] I would like to point out that our projects described in this book are always based on the genius loci as discussed in this book. The projects are however very different due to their situation, the relevant location, their typology, their scale, their utilization and the use of required technical means. In this context, I refer to the large-scale design for the town of Glatt.[2] The example clearly shows how different scales also require different strategies to fulfil climate demands.

[1] Haus Rauch. Ein Modell moderner Lehmarchitektur. R. Boltshauser, M. Rauch. Eds.: O. Kapfinger and A. Simon. Basel: Birkhäuser 2010, German/English

[2] Glatt! Manifest für eine Stadt im Werden. Authors: Boltshauser Architekten, EM2N, Frank Zierau Architekt, pool Architekten, Schweingruber Zulauf Landschaftsarchitekten. Ed.: Sascha Roesler. Zurich: Park Books, 2012.
The architectural group 'Krokodil' presents how urban density and the good mixture of uses it entails have a positive effect on the energy balance. The spatial proximity of different typologies and building standards forms the basis for exchanging and balancing out energy requirements and surpluses.

Building site, Haus Rauch (photo: Reinhold Ammann)

Simulation

Urs-Peter Menti, Christoph Stettler

While the strategies of measures present possible volumetric and spatial approaches in very different climate zones, this paragraph focuses on the temperate climate zone of central Europe. Unlike the planned or constructed examples presented above, primary design decisions are assessed here with respect to their energy effect using building simulations. The results are systematically presented using a structural study.

This study sorts the parameters that are important for all processes into thematic sections such as altitude, orientation, volumetrics, typology, materialisation, etc. In addition to underlying conditions that cannot be influenced, the presentation especially takes into account those that can be influenced, creating a "zoo"[1] of possible designs. Since residential use makes up 80 % of worldwide construction,[2] the focus of this study is on residential buildings. It should be considered that these results are only partially applicable to other types of use. Particular focus lies on the residential "block", which is widespread in Switzerland, as a semi-detached dwelling with eight apartments.

An apartment with an average 300 cubic metre volume (L x B x H = 10 x 10 x 3 metres) serves as the basic model. The block is used to change individual parameters and compare the results with the basic version. This assessment of early stages of conceptual design aims to determine which type of volume, building deformation, openings etc. are worthwhile with reference to energy efficiency and – compared to a simple cubic residential block – passive solar gains.

So strategies are sought to minimise the entire non-renewable energy demand ("primary energy demand n. r.") during the entire lifecycle of the building. The total primary energy demand n. r. here includes operative energy for room heating, room cooling and lighting, as well as embodied energy for the production, maintenance and disposal of the building.

[1] The term is regarded as ambiguous here. On the one hand it means the concentrated accumulation of species and on the other a dense combination with reference to the Zoo, which is in fact a compression program.

[2] Census 2000, Federal Statistical Office, Neuchâtel 2009. In: http://www.bfs.admin.ch/bfs/portal/de/i ndex/themen/09/02/blank/key/gebaeude/art und groesse.html, July 2, 2009

The following example shows how complex the effects of design decisions can be on the total primary energy demand n. r.: A balcony increases the shade on a façade in the summer and thereby reduces cooling requirements. But it also reduces gains from solar power in the winter, resulting in higher heating requirements. A balcony also reduces daylight use, which increases artificial light requirements and leads to higher embodied energy demand. So is a balcony advantageous or not from an overall energy perspective? To answer the question, the building becomes a complex system full of interaction that can only be sufficiently recorded and represented by means of simulations based on calculation models. Today's simulation instruments are able to record all forms of operative energy and optimise the ancillary conditions with respect to a defined value e. g. in this case to optimize the operative energy requirements of the overall primary energy demand n.r. Subsequently, well known, established, but also perhaps surprising structures are studied with respect to their (apparent) high energy efficiency in terms of overall heating, cooling and lighting. Energy demand for ventilation and appliances was deliberately not taken into account, since it is assumed that requirements for all studied variations would be similar when used in the same way. Various technological systems (e. g. elevators) are not included in calculations for the sake of simplicity. Embodied energy is calculated in parallel with operative energy. The sum of the non-renewable proportion of operative energy demand (primary energy n. r.) and the primary energy demand n. r. for producing, maintaining and disposing (= embodied energy) is also presented as the total primary energy demand n. r.

Starting with the basic version, the building is altered, whereby only one parameter is changed at a time.[3] The influence of this change on heating, cooling and lighting energy requirements on the level of usable energy is studied, as well as how the change affects the operative energy requirements on the level of primary energy n. r. Thus it quickly becomes apparent which changes have a significant effect on the operative energy requirements and where the effect is only marginal; and also where detailed analysis confirms prior experience and where new insight can be gained.

[3] Ceteris-Paribus Clause

[4] IDA ICE 4.0
[5] Operative periods, internal loads for lighting, people and equipment
[6] Temperatures, radiation, wind etc.

A computer program for "thermal building simulation" is used for the analyses.[4] In the simulation program, a detailed building model is created that takes into account the building geometry, the heat transmission and heat storage of all building elements, the building technology systems and their mode of operation, the use[5] and the external climate.[6] Typically in hourly increments over the course of one year, all of the building's energy flows including energy storage processes are calculated, allowing a forecast of how the building would behave in reality from an energy perspective. The resulting values from the simulation are for instance the indoor air temperature in individual rooms or – in the case of this study – operative energy requirements to constantly maintain the indoor air temperature within a range between 20.0 and 26.5°C and ensure sufficient lighting in those rooms. The cooling intended for the rooms in the simulation does not concur with tradition, since residential spaces in our latitudes do not typically require cooling. But it is necessary for comparison, in order to maintain the room conditions for all variants within a narrow band for a comfortable indoor air temperature. In reality, high cooling requirements indicate a room with partially high indoor air temperatures (if it is not cooled), which means a reduced thermal comfort. A lack of cooling requirements show that in appropriate buildings the temperature can be maintained in the required temperature range without much cooling effort.

As a result of experiences connected with the 1st edition of this publication, the simulations were adapted in a number of ways. The basic model of a residential block was rotated by 90° to allow a long side to face the south. The window proportions are no longer equal on all sides, and are instead altered depending on the direction in which the façade faces.

A new element is a window proportion of 60% for south-facing façades, of 40% for west and east-facing façades and 20% for northern façades. In the new basic version, the U-Value of the latest legal regulations for new buildings have been adopted. Another modification of the basic model is a structure placed on the outer walls to fulfil the SIA 380/1 (2009) limits (yet another version uses a structure that fulfils more stringent limits).

The analyzed variants were also adapted. The cladding has been replaced by a glazed balcony on the south side and the porosity (inner courtyard) has been completely dropped. An apartment building and an almost completely buried single-family home have also been added.
These and other (model-specific) adaptations make it impossible to directly compare the quantitative results of the 1st and 2nd editions. While embodied energy was only calculated for a few variants in the 1st edition, it is included as standard in all variants for the 2nd edition. Aditionally the total greenhouse gas emission of production, maintenance, disposal and operation is now presented.

Case Studies on Main Bodies

Christoph Stettler, Urs-Peter Menti, Serge Mattli, Dieter Lüthi

Simulations are a potent tool for architects and planners. They can be used to study the influence of aspects such as the location, orientation, scale, proportion, balconies, deformation, stepping, burying, the degree and the distribution of openings, covering and construction have on the primary energy requirements of a building (including the production, maintenance, disposal and operation).

Primary energy is the energy that is available in a naturally occurring form or source: e.g. uranium, coal, gas, geothermal energy, hydro-electric power, biomass, sun and wind. Primary energy is transformed into secondary energy through transformation processes (e.g. crude oil is refined to produce heating oil). Transporting secondary energy to the consumer results in transmission losses. The energy delivered to the consumer is known as final energy. Transformation processes transform final energy into used energy , for instance these might be heating oil or wood pellets. Further transformation processes turn the end energy into use energy (e.g. heating oil is combusted to create heat, or electricity is converted into light). The use energy is the energy available to the end user to provide the desired energy service.

Simulation can calculate the energy requirements for room heating, room cooling (use energy) and lighting (end energy). The former is converted into end energy demand using the performance data from the technical systems used and the level of use, before being converted to primary energy demand on the basis of energy-carrier-specific primary energy factors. The primary energy requirements are covered by renewable and non-renewable energy sources. The following considerations are limited to non-renewable primary energy demand (total primary energy demand n. r.), as is standard for normative study methods (SIA Merkblatt 2032, SIA Merkblatt 2040).

Key for diagrams

Assumed annual operation figures and conversion factors for additional cooling/heating performance and lighting:

		Primary energy factors (non-renewable)	Greenhouse gas emissions
		[kWh/kWh]	[kg CO_2/kWh]
Heating	Air/Water heat exchange pump: annual performance factor 2.8 Electricity: CH consumer mix	0.94	0.053
Cooling	Conventional cooling machine with air capacitor: annual performance factor 2.5 Electricity: CH consumer mix	1.05	0.059
Lighting	Electricity: CH consumer mix	2.63	0.148

(Storage and distribution losses ignored; Source: KBOB Ökobilanzdaten im Baubereich, 2009/1, Date July 2012)

The following calculations determine seven key figures and present them in absolute values: [kWh/m²a] or [kg CO_2/m²a]. With respect to the variations, the total primary energy demand n.r. is shown in relation to the basic version as a relative percentage value [%].

The following values are presented: Total primary energy demand n. r. compared to the basic version (in %)

Total primary energy demand n.r.: Operative energy demand + embodied energy[1] (each on the level of primary energy n.r. in [kWh/m²a])

Total greenhouse gas emissions (emissions produced in operation + embodied greenhouse gas emissions[2] in [kg CO_2/m²a])

Embodied energy (primary energy demand n.r. for production, maintenance and disposal in [kWh/m²a])

Operative energy demand (primary energy demand n.r. for room heating, room cooling and lighting; $Q_{tot\ Prim.\ n.\ r.}$ in [kWh/m²a])

Use energy demand for room heating (minimum room temperature 20.0°C; $Q_{Heating}$), room cooling (maximum room temperatures 26.5°C; $Q_{Cooling}$) and end energy demand for lighting (provision of sufficient lighting during use periods; $Q_{Lighting}$ in [kWh/m2a])

Marginal conditions: Use times and use conditions according to SIA 2024 (living). Form factor = Building shell area/building volume; a low form factor is typical of a compact building and indicates a large building volume with a comparatively low building shell area.

[1] Embodied energy is the total amount of non-renewable primary energy required for all prior processes, including extracting the raw materials, production and refining processes, and for disposal, including the required transports and equipment. It is described as a cumulative, non-renewable energy demand. (Source: SIA Merkblatt 2032) Calculations for the embodied energy of production, maintenance and disposal used calculation support provided by SIA 2040.

[2] Embodied greenhouse gas emissions describe the volume of greenhouse gases (CO_2, methane, nitrogen oxide and other gases that affect the climate) that are emitted during all prior processes, including raw material extraction, production, processing, maintenance and disposal, as well as the necessary transports and equipment. The same balance is taken into account as for embodied energy. (Source: SIA Merkblatt 2032)
Calculations for the embodied greenhouse gas emission of production, maintenance and disposal used calculation support provided by SIA 2040. Operative greenhouse gas emissions were calculated with the help of life cycle assessment data in the building industry. (Source: KBOB Ökobilanzdaten im Baubereich, 2009/1, July 2012)

Location

External climatic conditions (exterior air temperature, solar radiation) vary in view of the differing altitude of the object's possible location. Calculated locations: Basel (300 m above sea level), Zurich Meteoschweiz (600 m above sea level), Engelberg (1000 m above sea level), Davos (1500 m above sea level)

Conclusion

As expected, the change in the required lighting energy is only insignificant. Room cooling is gradually reduced to zero with increasing altitude. Heating energy requirements increase as the exterior temperature falls, and fall with increasing passive solar gains. From Zurich to Engelberg, the energy requirements for room heating increase massively. Interestingly, they fall in Davos compared to Engelberg due to considerably higher passive solar gains (with only slightly lower outside temperatures), reflecting the fact that Davos is the only location analysed here that is situated above the fog boundary.

300 mamsl

	91%	
Total primary energy n.r.	79	kWh/m^2a
Embodied energy	32	kWh/m^2a
Embodied greenhouse gas emissions	12	$kg\ CO_2/m^2a$
$Q_{tot\ Prim.\ n.\ r.}$	47	kWh/m^2a
$Q_{Heating}$	28	kWh/m^2a
$Q_{Cooling}$	1	kWh/m^2a
$Q_{Lighting}$	8	kWh/m^2a
Form factor	0.47	

U-Value: building shell and windows

The basic version's building shell has the following U-Value: opaque building elements 0.2 W/m^2K, 3 IV glass with 0.7 W/m^2K, frame 1.2 W/m^2K (85 % glass, 15 % frame). The thermal quality of the building shell is on the one hand worsened (opaque elements 0.2 W/m^2K, 2 IV glass with 1.1 W/m^2K, frame 1.4 W/m^2K) and on the other hand improved (roof 0.09 W/m^2K, wall/floor 0.11 W/m^2K, 3 IV glass with 0.7 W/m^2K, frame 1.2 W/m^2K). The basic version represents a standard building with 3 IV windows, while the version with a worse building shell is a building that complies with legal standards. The version with an improved building shell conforms to "Minergie P" standards.

Conclusion

The energy requirements for lighting hardly change. Energy demand for room cooling can be ignored in all cases. Energy requirements for room heating dominate operative energy demand in the winter months and react most to changes, since a well-insulated shell can above all prevent the building from cooling down at night. Due to the very good insulation of the building shell, the nocturnal cooling effect on the building in the summer could not be registered for the residential use studied here.

U-Value

Glass:

Frame:

Opaque building elements:

Energy transmittance

Glass:

Total primary energy n. r.

Embodied energy

Embodied greenhouse gas emissions

$Q_{tot\ Prim.\ n.\ r.}$

$Q_{Heating}$

$Q_{Cooling}$

$Q_{Lighting}$

Form factor

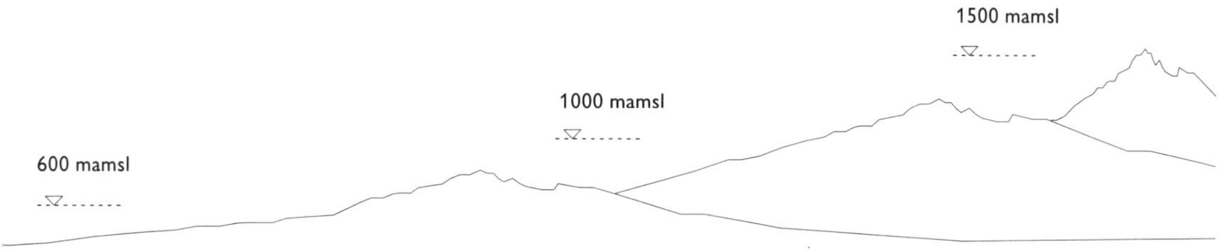

Basic version

100%		**109%**		**104%**	
87	kWh/m^{2}a	95	kWh/m^{2}a	90	kWh/m^{2}a
32	kWh/m^{2}a	32	kWh/m^{2}a	32	kWh/m^{2}a
12	kg CO_2/m^{2}a	12	kg CO_2/m^{2}a	12	kg CO_2/m^{2}a
55	kWh/m^{2}a	63	kWh/m^{2}a	58	kWh/m^{2}a
36	kWh/m^{2}a	43	kWh/m^{2}a	41	kWh/m^{2}a
0	kWh/m^{2}a	0	kWh/m^{2}a	0	kWh/m^{2}a
8	kWh/m^{2}a	8	kWh/m^{2}a	8	kWh/m^{2}a
0.47		0.47		0.47	

Limit with window 2 IV		Limit with window 3 IV		Target with window 3 IV	
100%		**100%**		**92%**	
1.1	W/m^{2}K	0.7	W/m^{2}K	0.7	W/m^{2}K
1.4	W/m^{2}K	1.2	W/m^{2}K	1.2	W/m^{2}K
0.2	W/m^{2}K	0.2	W/m^{2}K	0.1	W/m^{2}K
60	%	48	%	48	%
87	kWh/m^{2}a	87	kWh/m^{2}a	80	kWh/m^{2}a
31	kWh/m^{2}a	32	kWh/m^{2}a	32	kWh/m^{2}a
12	kg CO_2/m^{2}a	12	kg CO_2/m^{2}a	12	kg CO_2/m^{2}a
57	kWh/m^{2}a	55	kWh/m^{2}a	48	kWh/m^{2}a
37	kWh/m^{2}a	36	kWh/m^{2}a	28	kWh/m^{2}a
0	kWh/m^{2}a	0	kWh/m^{2}a	0	kWh/m^{2}a
8	kWh/m^{2}a	8	kWh/m^{2}a	8	kWh/m^{2}a
0.47		0.47		0.47	

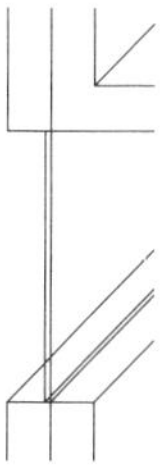

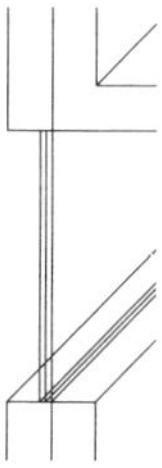

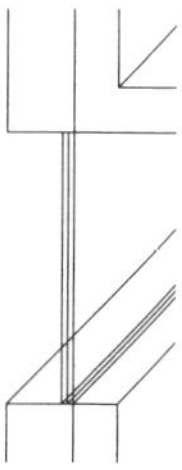

Deformation I

Compared to the basic version, a west façade has one concave and one convex deformation. The building volume therefore remains the same.

Conclusion

Energy requirements for room cooling and lighting do not change significantly. Convex deformation can slightly reduce the energy requirements for room heating, since the exterior surface area is slightly smaller (approaching a semi-circular shape, which represents the lowest possible form factor) and also slightly higher passive solar gains are achieved due to the slightly more ideal façade area facing the sun. The lower form factor also leads to a (very) slight reduction in embodied energy.

Concave deformation leads to higher energy demand for room heating (greater development, more self-shading). The higher form factor results in a slightly higher embodied energy demand.

Total primary energy n.r.
Embodied energy
Embodied greenhouse gas emissions
$Q_{tot\ Prim.\ n.\ r.}$
$Q_{Heating}$
$Q_{Cooling}$
$Q_{Lighting}$
Form factor

Deformation II

In the basic version, the façades are equally large on the south and north sides. On that basis, with the same window proportions, the building is opened once to the north and once to the south (north façade three times as large as the south façade and vice versa).

Conclusion

Energy requirements for lighting do not significantly change. That confirms that the daylight use in residential buildings is mostly sufficient due to the small room depths and the low lighting requirements compared to functional buildings. Enlarging the southern façade leads to an increase in energy requirements for room cooling. The room heating demand changes especially when the south façade shrinks and the north façade grows.

The initially expected positive effect on passive solar gains by opening the south side does not occur. From a purely geometric perspective, enlarging the south façade makes the east and west façades tend to become north-east and north-west façades. The additional gains on the south façade are cancelled out by the reduced gains on the east and west façades. The same phenomenon can be seen when enlarging the north façade, which generally has low gain levels: The east and west façades become south-east and south-west façades with accordingly increased passive solar gains. At the same time, the longer development (higher form factor) increases U-Value losses.

Total primary energy n.r.
Embodied energy
Embodied greenhouse gas emissions
$Q_{tot\ Prim.\ n.\ r.}$
$Q_{Heating}$
$Q_{Cooling}$
$Q_{Lighting}$
Form factor

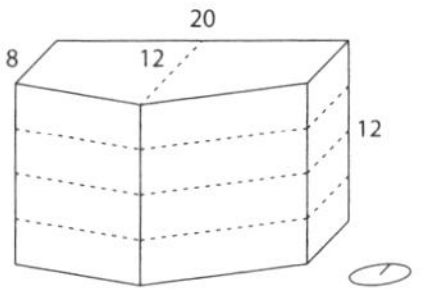

South façade, Convex

99%

86 kWh/m^{2}a
32 kWh/m^{2}a
12 kg CO_2/m^{2}a
55 kWh/m^{2}a
35 kWh/m^{2}a
0 kWh/m^{2}a
8 kWh/m^{2}a
0.45

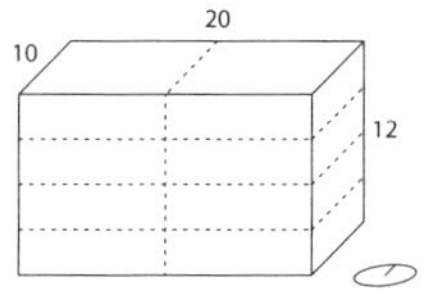

Basic version

100%

87 kWh/m^{2}a
32 kWh/m^{2}a
12 kg CO_2/m^{2}a
55 kWh/m^{2}a
36 kWh/m^{2}a
0 kWh/m^{2}a
8 kWh/m^{2}a
0.47

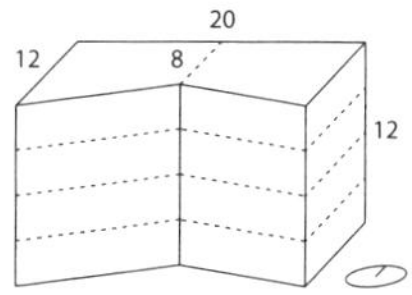

South façade, Concave

103%

90 kWh/m^{2}a
33 kWh/m^{2}a
12 kg CO_2/m^{2}a
57 kWh/m^{2}a
38 kWh/m^{2}a
0 kWh/m^{2}a
8 kWh/m^{2}a
0.49

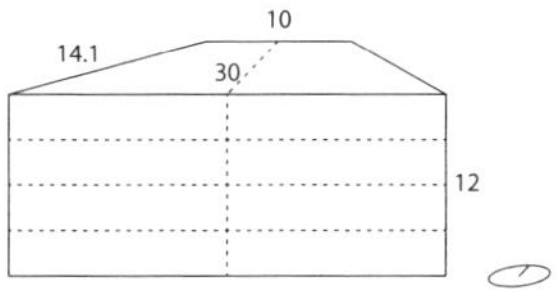

Trapeze south

103%

90 kWh/m^{2}a
34 kWh/m^{2}a
13 kg CO_2/m^{2}a
55 kWh/m^{2}a
37 kWh/m^{2}a
1 kWh/m^{2}a
8 kWh/m^{2}a
0.51

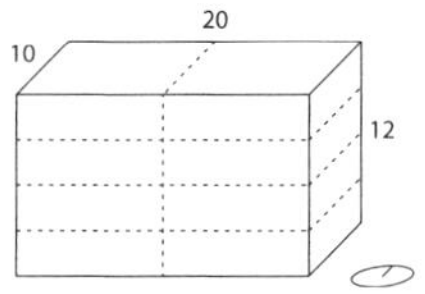

Basic version

100%

87 kWh/m^{2}a
32 kWh/m^{2}a
12 kg CO_2/m^{2}a
55 kWh/m^{2}a
36 kWh/m^{2}a
0 kWh/m^{2}a
8 kWh/m^{2}a
0.47

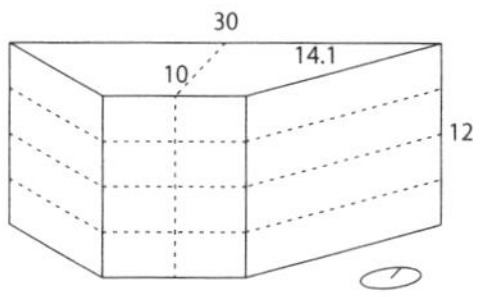

Trapeze north

103%

90 kWh/m^{2}a
33 kWh/m^{2}a
12 kg CO_2/m^{2}a
57 kWh/m^{2}a
38 kWh/m^{2}a
0 kWh/m^{2}a
8 kWh/m^{2}a
0.51

Steps

The buildings are given steps on one side and both sides.

Conclusion

Lighting energy demand is slightly lower with single side steps. The heating requirements increase with the increasing number of steps. The cooling requirements are negligible. Operative energy demand is dominated by room heating requirements, which increase in relation to the amount of steps. Steps lead to an increased form factor, which in turn increases the transmittance losses and had a negative effect on the room heating energy demand. Passive solar gains achieved by the steps may weaken that effect somewhat, but cannot compensate for the increased losses. Embodied energy increases with an increasing form factor (i. e. more steps).

Total primary energy n.r.
Embodied energy
Embodied greenhouse gas emissions
$Q_{tot\ Prim.\ n.\ r.}$
$Q_{Heating}$
$Q_{Cooling}$
$Q_{Lighting}$
Form factor

Orientation

An eight-family building as a basic version with a main façade towards the south is rotated once by 45°, 90°, 180°, 270° and 315°.

Conclusion

Here too, the dominant factors for operative energy requirements are changes in energy demand for room heating. There is no demand for room cooling. Energy demand for lighting remains unchanged. U-Value losses are the same for all versions because the sum of the window areas does not change. Uneven distribution of the windows on different façades however, combined with a rotation of the volume, does lead to differently exposed window areas depending on their direction. That causes different passive solar gains. As expected, a high proportion of windows towards the south and a low window proportion towards the north produces ideal room heating energy demand. The more the actual south façade window areas are rotated towards the north, the higher the energy demand for room heating.

If the sensitivity study with respect to orientation is carried out for a building with 40 residential units and a form factor of 0.81, significantly lower changes occur, because the specific U-Value losses and solar gains are lower per unit of living space.

Total primary energy n.r.
Embodied energy
Embodied greenhouse gas emissions
$Q_{tot\ Prim.\ n.\ r.}$
$Q_{Heating}$
$Q_{Cooling}$
$Q_{Lighting}$
Form factor

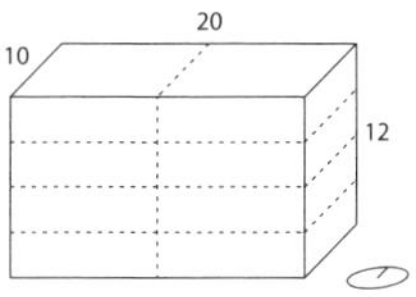

Basic version

100%

87 kWh/m²a
32 kWh/m²a
12 kg CO_2/m²a
55 kWh/m²a
36 kWh/m²a
0 kWh/m²a
8 kWh/m²a
0.47

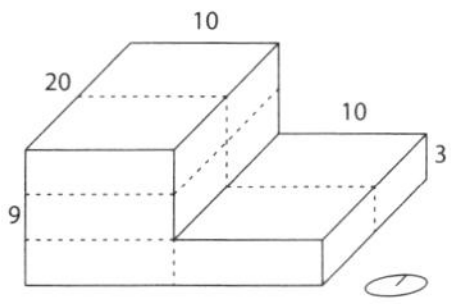

Single-sided stepping

113%

99 kWh/m²a
33 kWh/m²a
13 kg CO_2/m²a
65 kWh/m²a
46 kWh/m²a
0 kWh/m²a
8 kWh/m²a
0.58

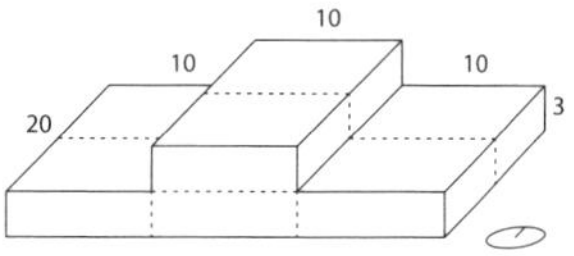

Double-sided stepping

125%

109 kWh/m²a
36 kWh/m²a
14 kg CO_2/m²a
73 kWh/m²a
52 kWh/m²a
0 kWh/m²a
9 kWh/m²a
0.7

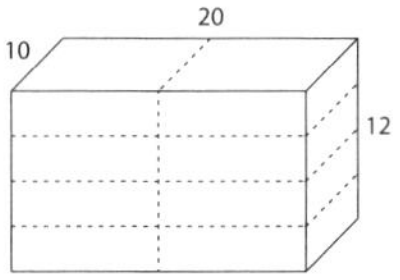

Basic version 0° (South)

100%

87 kWh/m²a
32 kWh/m²a
12 kg CO_2/m²a
55 kWh/m²a
36 kWh/m²a
0 kWh/m²a
8 kWh/m²a
0.47

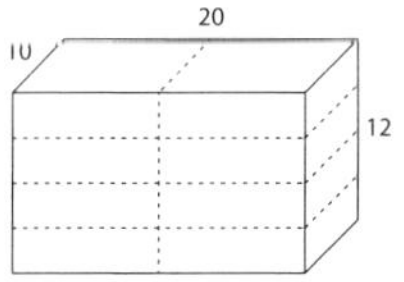

45° (Southeast)

103%

90 kWh/m²a
32 kWh/m²a
12 kg CO_2/m²a
58 kWh/m²a
38 kWh/m²a
0 kWh/m²a
8 kWh/m²a
0.47

102%

89 kWh/m²a
32 kWh/m²a
12 kg CO_2/m²a
57 kWh/m²a
39 kWh/m²a
0 kWh/m²a
8 kWh/m²a
0.47

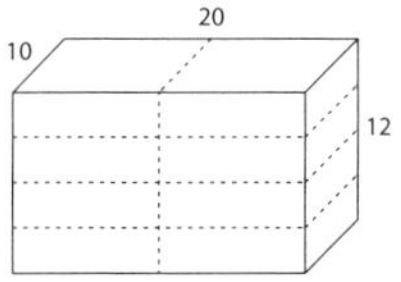

315° (Southwest)

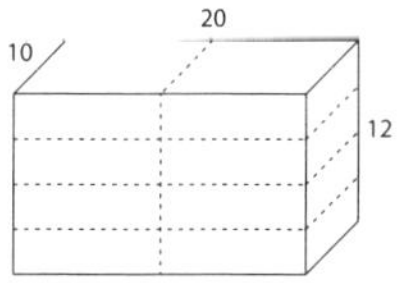

90° (East)

107%

93 kWh/m²a
32 kWh/m²a
12 kg CO_2/m²a
61 kWh/m²a
41 kWh/m²a
0 kWh/m²a
8 kWh/m²a
0.47

106%

92 kWh/m²a
32 kWh/m²a
12 kg CO_2/m²a
60 kWh/m²a
42 kWh/m²a
0 kWh/m²a
8 kWh/m²a
0.47

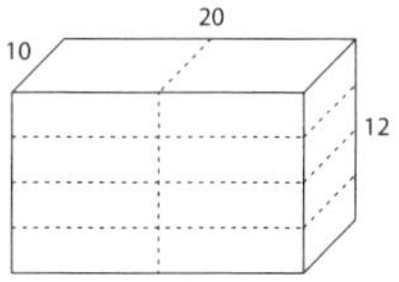

270° (West)

109%

95 kWh/m²a
32 kWh/m²a
12 kg CO_2/m²a
63 kWh/m²a
44 kWh/m²a
0 kWh/m²a
8 kWh/m²a
0.47

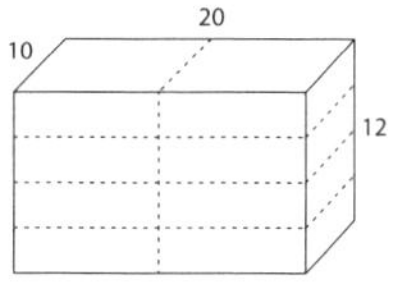

180° (North)

Window distribution

The distribution of window areas (basic version: S 60%, W/E 40%, N 20%) is changed (S 80%, W/E 30%, N 10%). These window proportions are rotated three times by 90 respectively.

Conclusion

As expected, the energy requirements for room heating fall with larger window proportions on the south façade and rise when the window proportion falls. The energy demand for room cooling and lighting hardly has an influence.

	Basic version	0°
N	20%	10%
E	40%	30%
S	60%	80%
W	40%	30%

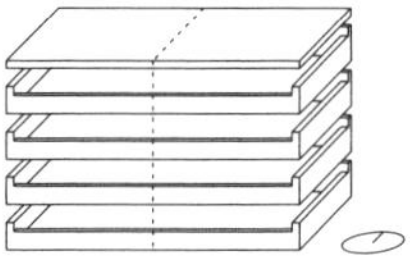

Basic version

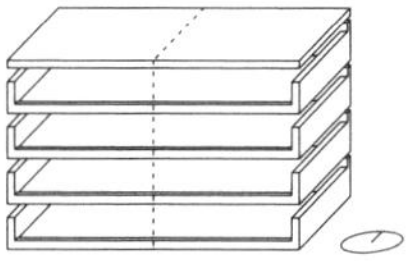

0°

	100%	**97%**
Total primary energy n.r.	87 kWh/m²a	84 kWh/m²a
Embodied energy	32 kWh/m²a	32 kWh/m²a
Embodied greenhouse gas emissions	12 kg CO_2/m²a	12 kg CO_2/m²a
$Q_{tot\ Prim.\ n.\ r.}$	55 kWh/m²a	52 kWh/m²a
$Q_{Heating}$	36 kWh/m²a	33 kWh/m²a
$Q_{Cooling}$	0 kWh/m²a	0 kWh/m²a
$Q_{Lighting}$	8 kWh/m²a	8 kWh/m²a
Form factor	0.47	0.47

Aperture proportion

The entire window proportion of the façades is varied between 20%, 50% and 80%. The basic version has an approximate aperture proportion of 40%.

Conclusion

An average aperture proportion of 50% is ideal with respect to the total primary energy demand n. r. It is beneficial to distribute window areas unevenly depending on the direction they face (N, O, S, W). To maximise passive solar gains, the windows facing the south side should tend to be large, while the windows to the north should tend to be small, thereby minimising U-Value losses. Windows facing the east and west have the greatest influence on energy demand for cooling (low sun position). The most important consideration in this respect is that exterior sun shielding prevents too high solar warming in the summer (and therefore increased energy demand for room cooling). A window proportion of 50% leads to sufficient daylight use. A higher window proportion only slightly improves daylight use, but also leads to a strong increase in embodied energy.

Total primary energy n.r.
Embodied energy
Embodied greenhouse gas emissions
$Q_{tot\ Prim.\ n.\ r.}$
$Q_{Heating}$
$Q_{Cooling}$
$Q_{Lighting}$
Form factor

N 30%
E 10%
S 30%
W 80%

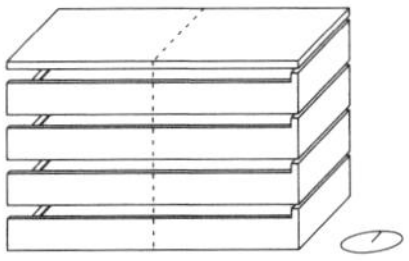

90°

108%

94 kWh/m^2a
32 kWh/m^2a
12 $kg\ CO_2/m^2a$
62 kWh/m^2a
43 kWh/m^2a
0 kWh/m^2a
8 kWh/m^2a
0.47

N 80%
E 30%
S 10%
W 30%

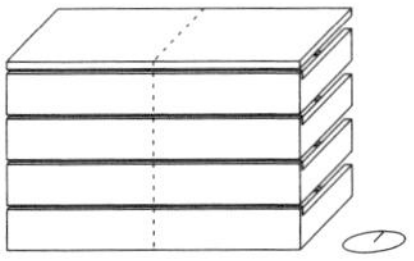

180°

112%

98 kWh/m^2a
32 kWh/m^2a
13 $kg\ CO_2/m^2a$
66 kWh/m^2a
47 kWh/m^2a
1 kWh/m^2a
8 kWh/m^2a
0.47

N 30%
E 80%
S 30%
W 10%

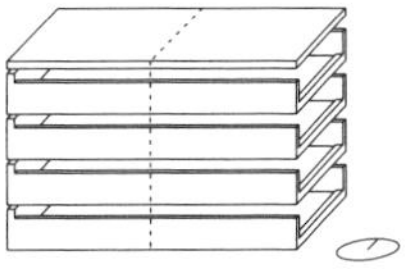

270°

106%

92 kWh/m^2a
32 kWh/m^2a
12 $kg\ CO_2/m^2a$
60 kWh/m^2a
41 kWh/m^2a
0 kWh/m^2a
8 kWh/m^2a
0.47

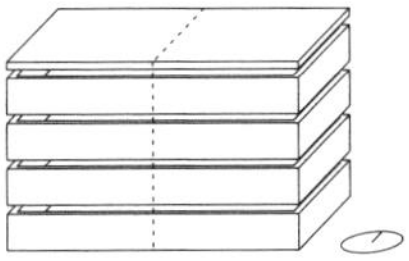

20% aperture

107%

94 kWh/m^2a
30 kWh/m^2a
12 $kg\ CO_2/m^2a$
64 kWh/m^2a
42 kWh/m^2a
0 kWh/m^2a
9 kWh/m^2a
0.47

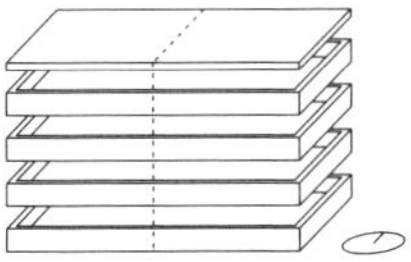

50% aperture

105%

91 kWh/m^2a
33 kWh/m^2a
12 $kg\ CO_2/m^2a$
58 kWh/m^2a
39 kWh/m^2a
1 kWh/m^2a
8 kWh/m^2a
0.47

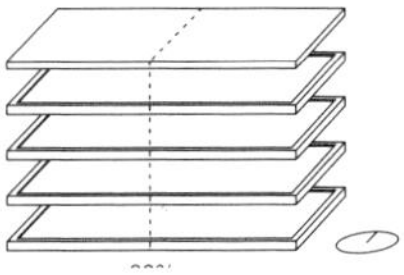

80% aperture

112%

98 kWh/m^2a
37 kWh/m^2a
13 $kg\ CO_2/m^2a$
61 kWh/m^2a
39 kWh/m^2a
5 kWh/m^2a
7 kWh/m^2a
0.47

Balcony

Starting with the basic version (without a surrounding balcony), a 2 m, 4 m and 6 m deep balcony was added to the south, west and east façades respectively.

Conclusion

The balconies reduce the daylight use and passive solar gains. The latter results in increased energy demand for room heating in relation to the increasing depth of the balcony. Because the windows have good, flexible sun protection, thereby keeping the energy requirements for room cooling low or non-existent, balconies do not produce any improvement.

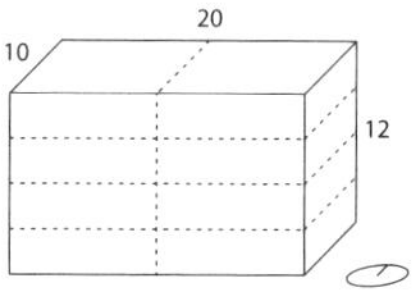

Basic version without balcony

100%

Total primary energy n.r.	87	kWh/m^2a
Embodied energy	32	kWh/m^2a
Embodied greenhouse gas emissions	12	$kg\ CO_2/m^2a$
$Q_{tot\ Prim.\ n.\ r.}$	55	kWh/m^2a
$Q_{Heating}$	36	kWh/m^2a
$Q_{Cooling}$	0	kWh/m^2a
$Q_{Lighting}$	8	kWh/m^2a
Form factor	0.47	

Glass-covered balcony

The balcony is attached to the south or north side, has a depth of 3 m and is covered with glass on all three sides. The glazing can be opened to prevent overheating in the summer.

Conclusion

If the balcony is covered with glass, the operative energy demand improves. Passive solar gains fall even further, but the U-Value losses are significantly reduced, thereby reducing room heating energy demand. Lighting energy requirements hardly change. Interestingly, a glass-covered balcony on the north side is better from an energy perspective than a glass-covered balcony on the south side. It has hardly any disadvantages, but a number of benefits. However the glazing increases the embodied energy to such an extent that with respect to overall primary energy demand n. r., a balcony always leads to worse results than versions without a balcony.

Total primary energy n.r.
Embodied energy
Embodied greenhouse gas emissions
$Q_{tot\ Prim.\ n.\ r.}$
$Q_{Heating}$
$Q_{Cooling}$
$Q_{Lighting}$
Form factor

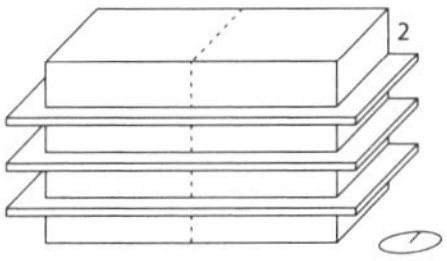

2 m balcony

111%

97	kWh/m^{2}a
33	kWh/m^{2}a
13	kg CO_2/m^{2}a
64	kWh/m^{2}a
44	kWh/m^{2}a
0	kWh/m^{2}a
8	kWh/m^{2}a
0.47	

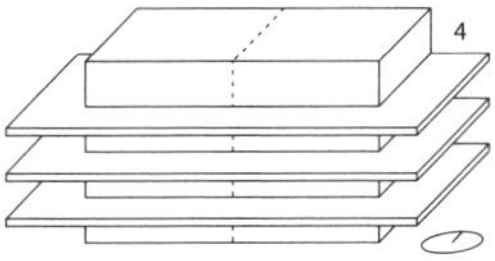

4 m balcony

118%

102	kWh/m^{2}a
34	kWh/m^{2}a
13	kg CO_2/m^{2}a
69	kWh/m^{2}a
49	kWh/m^{2}a
0	kWh/m^{2}a
9	kWh/m^{2}a
0.47	

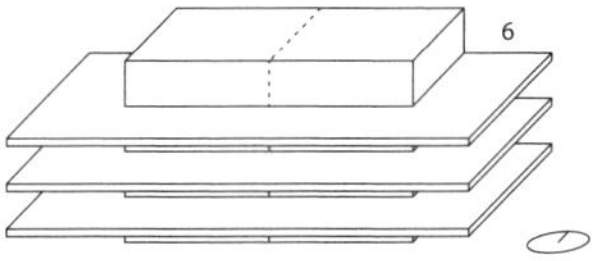

6 m balcony

120%

105	kWh/m^{2}a
35	kWh/m^{2}a
14	kg CO_2/m^{2}a
70	kWh/m^{2}a
50	kWh/m^{2}a
0	kWh/m^{2}a
9	kWh/m^{2}a
0.47	

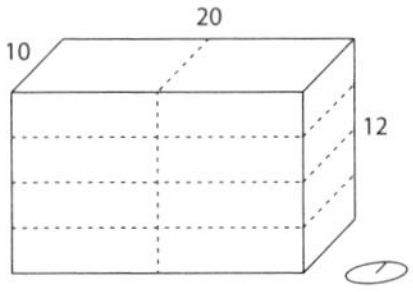

Basic version without balcony

100%

87	kWh/m^{2}a
32	kWh/m^{2}a
12	kg CO_2/m^{2}a
55	kWh/m^{2}a
36	kWh/m^{2}a
0	kWh/m^{2}a
8	kWh/m^{2}a
0.47	

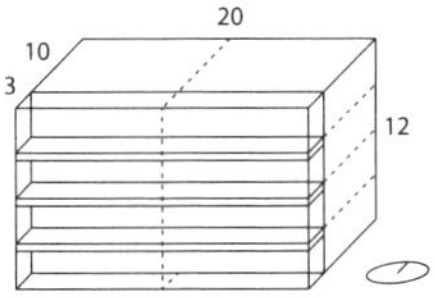

Glazed balcony to the south

117%

102	kWh/m^{2}a
39	kWh/m^{2}a
14	kg CO_2/m^{2}a
63	kWh/m^{2}a
43	kWh/m^{2}a
0	kWh/m^{2}a
9	kWh/m^{2}a
0.47	

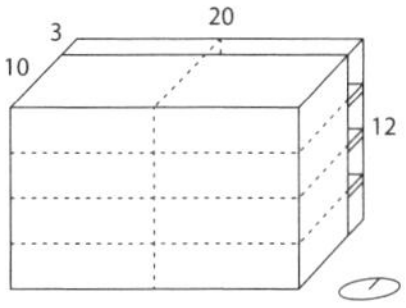

Glazed balcony to the north

107%

94	kWh/m^{2}a
39	kWh/m^{2}a
14	kg CO_2/m^{2}a
54	kWh/m^{2}a
35	kWh/m^{2}a
0	kWh/m^{2}a
8	kWh/m^{2}a
0.47	

Scale

Starting with the basic version of an apartment building with eight residential units, the single-family home on the one hand and versions with 24, 40 and 80 residential units on the other were simulated.

Conclusion

The room heating energy requirements significantly fall when switching from a single family home to an apartment building and reach a minimum in the case of 80 apartments. Lighting energy requirements continuously increase from a single family home to the largest apartment building, albeit to a moderate degree. Room cooling energy is not required in all versions.

Compact building (low form factor) is energy-efficient in residential building, both with respect to the operative energy demand and the embodied energy. Compared to apartment buildings, lighting and cooling play a minor role. The single family home is inefficient in all aspects of energy (operation, embodied energy).

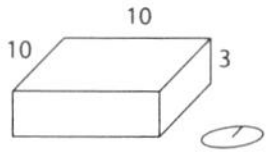

Single family home

152%

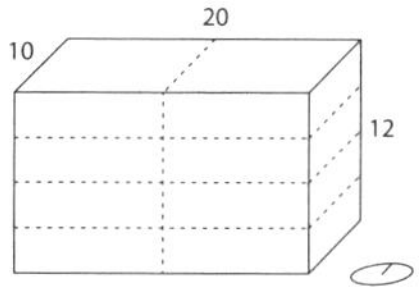

Basic version 8 apartments

100%

	Single family home	Basic version 8 apartments
Total primary energy n.r.	132 kWh/m^2a	87 kWh/m^2a
Embodied energy	47 kWh/m^2a	32 kWh/m^2a
Embodied greenhouse gas emissions	16 kg CO_2/m^2a	12 kg CO_2/m^2a
$Q_{tot\ Prim.\ n.\ r.}$	85 kWh/m^2a	55 kWh/m^2a
$Q_{Heating}$	69 kWh/m^2a	36 kWh/m^2a
$Q_{Cooling}$	0 kWh/m^2a	0 kWh/m^2a
$Q_{Lighting}$	8 kWh/m^2a	8 kWh/m^2a
Form factor	1.07	0.47

Proportion

The eight apartments are aligned in different directions.

Conclusion

Flat alignment – which quasi conforms to 8 terraced single family homes – performs significantly worse in terms of heating energy requirements compared to the other two compact versions. However cooling energy is also not required in this version. Lighting energy requirements are marginal. The embodied energy demand is significantly higher in the case of flat alignment than with more compact versions. This example again shows that compact buildings are sensible for residential development to keep the dominant room heating energy requirements low. The daylight use in compact buildings only slightly worsens.

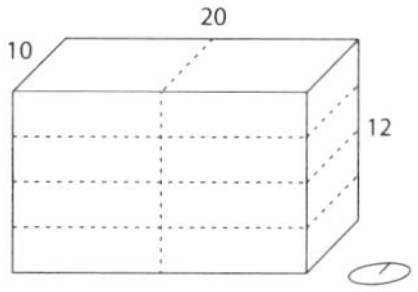

20m x 10m x 12m / Basic version

100%

	20m x 10m x 12m / Basic version
Total primary energy n.r.	87 kWh/m^2a
Embodied energy	32 kWh/m^2a
Embodied greenhouse gas emissions	12 kg CO_2/m^2a
$Q_{tot\ Prim.\ n.\ r.}$	55 kWh/m^2a
$Q_{Heating}$	36 kWh/m^2a
$Q_{Cooling}$	0 kWh/m^2a
$Q_{Lighting}$	8 kWh/m^2a
Form factor	0.47

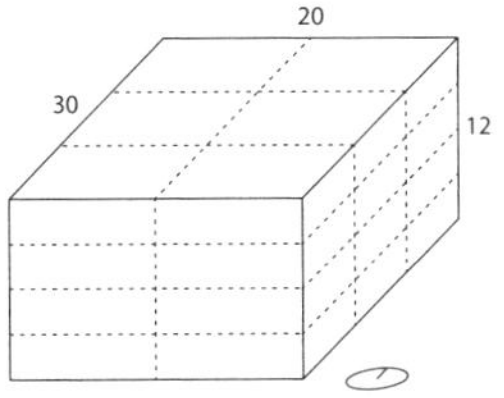

24 apartments

96%

84 kWh/m^{2}a
27 kWh/m^{2}a
11 kg CO_2/m^{2}a
57 kWh/m^{2}a
34 kWh/m^{2}a
0 kWh/m^{2}a
9 kWh/m^{2}a
0.33

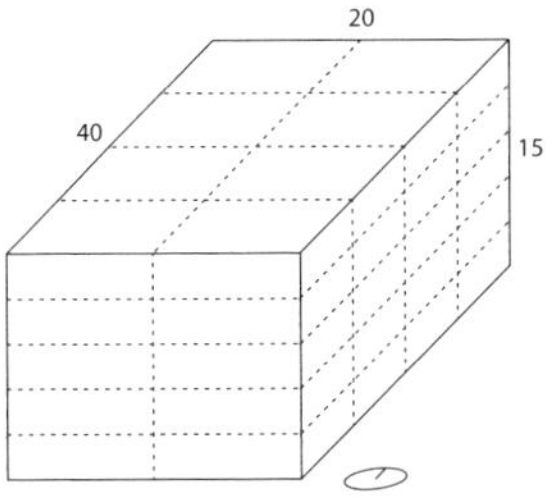

40 apartments

93%

81 kWh/m^{2}a
26 kWh/m^{2}a
10 kg CO_2/m^{2}a
56 kWh/m^{2}a
32 kWh/m^{2}a
0 kWh/m^{2}a
10 kWh/m^{2}a
0.28

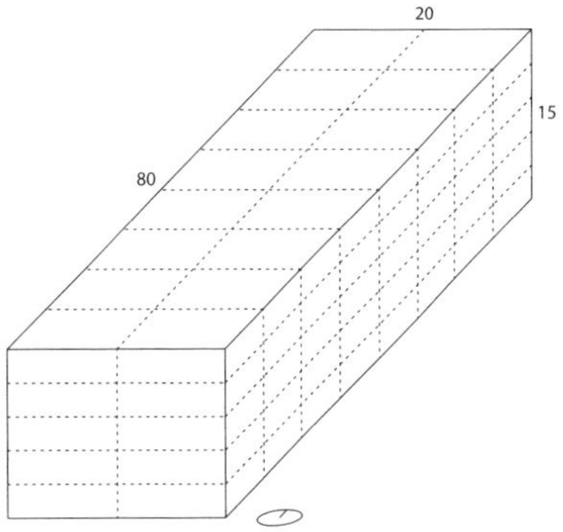

80 apartments

93%

81 kWh/m^{2}a
25 kWh/m^{2}a
10 kg CO_2/m^{2}a
56 kWh/m^{2}a
31 kWh/m^{2}a
0 kWh/m^{2}a
10 kWh/m^{2}a
0.26

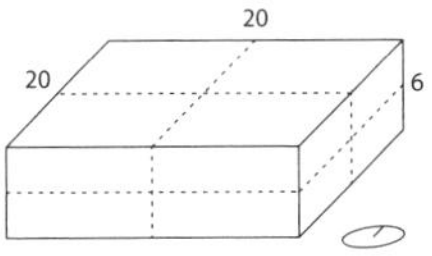

20m x 20m x 6m

110%

96 kWh/m^{2}a
32 kWh/m^{2}a
12 kg CO_2/m^{2}a
63 kWh/m^{2}a
43 kWh/m^{2}a
0 kWh/m^{2}a
9 kWh/m^{2}a
0.53

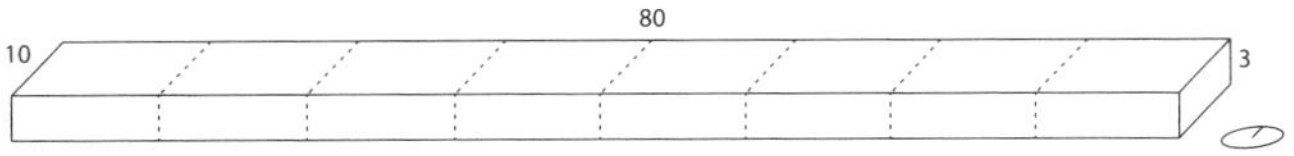

80m x 10m x 3m

136%

118 kWh/m^{2}a
41 kWh/m^{2}a
16 kg CO_2/m^{2}a
77 kWh/m^{2}a
58 kWh/m^{2}a
0 kWh/m^{2}a
9 kWh/m^{2}a
0.97

Construction

The (solid) basic version is compared to two versions using mixed construction types and one lightweight construction version.

Conclusion

Hardly any operative energy differences occur between the basic version and the first variation (mixed construction with AW=L, IW and ZD = MA).[1] The embodied energy is lower however in the case of lightweight building. In the other two versions with relatively lighter constructions, the energy demand for room heating rises significantly. The same applies to room cooling: The versions with a high degree of lightweight construction are among the few versions that require any energy at all for room cooling. As expected, lighting energy requirements remain unchanged in all versions. Thermally activated building mass strongly influences the energy demand of a building. If the roof, floors and suspended ceilings are massive, that already covers a large proportion of the mass required for energy-efficient operation. It is no longer decisive whether the exterior walls are massive or not. The lower amount of embodied energy in lightweight buildings is more than compensated by the increase in heating energy demand. In addition to the advantage of solid construction types in terms of energy demand for room heating and cooling, the lower performance requirements for room heating and cooling is also highly significant, since system sizes and the investment they entail can be reduced in this way.
All in all, buildings with a massive core, massive floors and ceilings, and lightweight exterior walls achieve best primary energy demand n. r. results.

[1] AW: exterior wall, IW: interior wall, ZD: partition walls

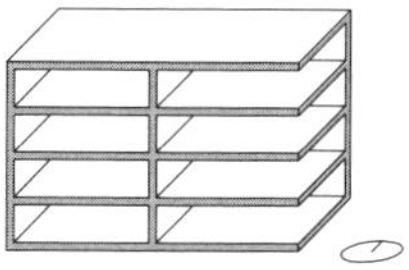

Solid basic version

100%

87	kWh/m²a
32	kWh/m²a
12	kg CO_2/m²a
55	kWh/m²a
36	kWh/m²a
0	kWh/m²a
8	kWh/m²a
0.47	

Buried single family home

Free-standing single family homes are covered with earth on all sides except for the south side.

Conclusion

The room heating energy demand falls significantly and the lighting energy requirements are increased. Despite the burying, the single family home performs worse than the basic version with 8 residential units with respect to primary energy demand n. r.

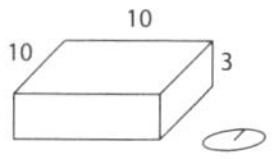

Basic version single family home

152%

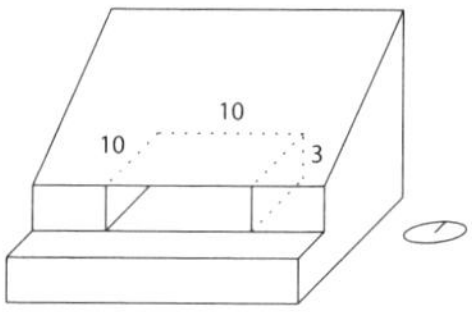

Single family home embedded on 5 sides

124%

	Basic version single family home	Single family home embedded on 5 sides
Total primary energy n.r.	132 kWh/m²a	108 kWh/m²a
Embodied energy	47 kWh/m²a	37 kWh/m²a
Embodied greenhouse gas emissions	16 kg CO_2/m²a	14 kg CO_2/m²a
$Q_{tot\ Prim.\ n.\ r.}$	85 kWh/m²a	72 kWh/m²a
$Q_{Heating}$	69 kWh/m²a	50 kWh/m²a
$Q_{Cooling}$	0 kWh/m²a	0 kWh/m²a
$Q_{Lighting}$	8 kWh/m²a	9 kWh/m²a
Form factor	1.07	1.07

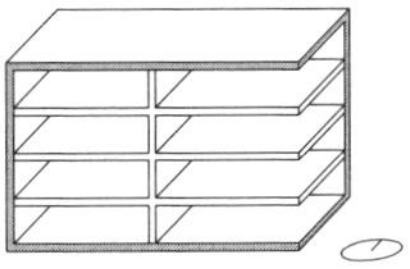

Lightweight intermediate ceilings and interior walls

103%

90	kWh/m²a
31	kWh/m²a
12	kg CO_2/m²a
59	kWh/m²a
39	kWh/m²a
1	kWh/m²a
8	kWh/m²a
0.47	

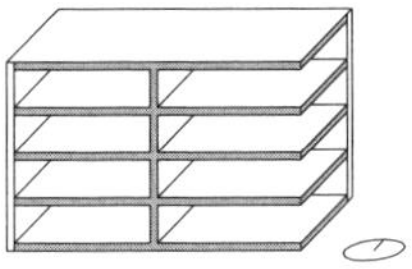

Lightweight exterior wall

97%

85	kWh/m²a
30	kWh/m²a
11	kg CO_2/m²a
55	kWh/m²a
36	kWh/m²a
0	kWh/m²a
8	kWh/m²a
0.47	

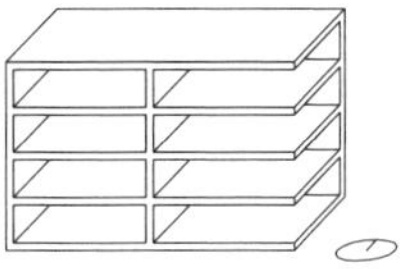

Lightweight construction

102%

89	kWh/m²a
28	kWh/m²a
11	kg CO_2/m²a
60	kWh/m²a
40	kWh/m²a
1	kWh/m²a
8	kWh/m²a
0.47	

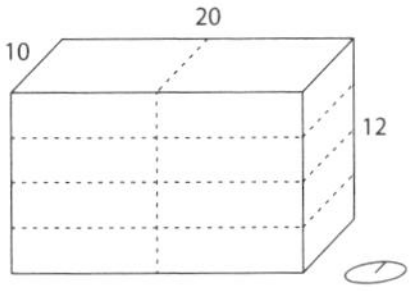

Basic version

100%

87	kWh/m²a
32	kWh/m²a
12	kg CO_2/m²a
55	kWh/m²a
36	kWh/m²a
0	kWh/m²a
8	kWh/m²a
0.47	

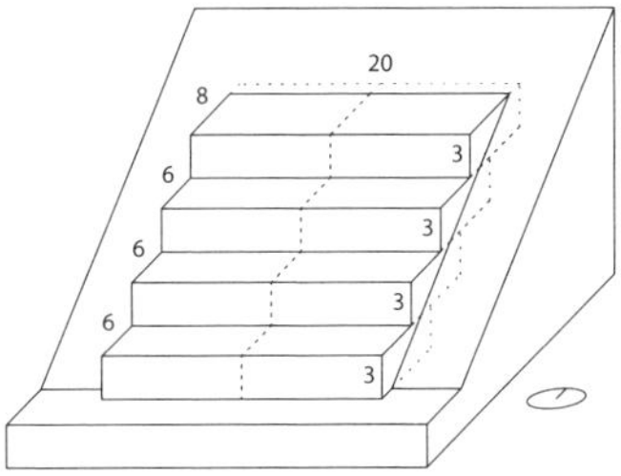

Apartment building 50% embedded

119%

104	kWh/m²a
39	kWh/m²a
14	kg CO_2/m²a
65	kWh/m²a
44	kWh/m²a
0	kWh/m²a
9	kWh/m²a
0.77	

Buried apartment building

The basic version is built as a (stepped) apartment building on a slope. 50% of the surface is covered by earth. The east and west façades have only 20% window proportions, while the north has 0%.

Conclusion

U-Value losses are reduced because 50% of the surfaces are beneath the earth. Nevertheless, the room heating energy demand rises because the stepped individual storeys lead to a considerably larger building shell area and therefore to increased U-Value loss. The reduced window surfaces also increased lighting energy demand. With respect to embodied energy, the greater excavation volumes also lead to worse results. From an energy perspective, burying a multi-storey apartment building is inefficient in all aspects.

Result

The case studies show that in residential building, the energy demand for space heating still plays a dominant role – even if the building is very well insulated. Embodied energy has a similar volume and must always be considered in a holistic assessment. The energy demand for lighting and room cooling plays a subordinate role in residential buildings.

Compact building types have a positive effect on heating energy requirements and on embodied energy. Since – unlike functional buildings perhaps – residential buildings with a compact form have no disadvantages in terms of daylight use or the energy requirements for room cooling, it can be concluded that a compact building is also a more energy-efficient building. This is confirmed by studies on scale, deformation, proportion and gradation. We can also conclude that massive building methods have considerable advantages in terms of the operative energy demand, even though the embodied energy is considerably increased. The lower operative energy demands can compensate for the increased embodied energy requirements. However simulations show that the thermally effective mass need not be maximised to the limit to achieve great efficiency; parts of the building can still consist of a lightweight structure.

Deformations are architecturally attractive, but not useful in terms of energy; as a range of examples show, they can even be counterproductive in that respect. That also applies to burying, which can only be achieved at the expense of a compact volume in the case of apartment buildings at least. Burying is only advantageous for single-family homes – but single-family homes are inefficient per se with respect to operative and embodied energy.

The proportion of windows has a major influence on the entire primary energy demand. It is evident that a window proportion of approximately 50 % is important for good daylight use and sufficient passive solar extraction. A higher proportion of windows primarily leads to high embodied energy and also to higher cooling requirements, while daylight use and passive solar extraction are not significantly better than a version with a 50 % window proportion. The distribution of the windows on the different façades is just as important as their proportion. As expected, a higher proportion of windows on the south façade (thereby maximising passive solar extraction) and a lower proportion of windows on the northern façade (minimising transmission heat loss) is generally sensible.

From the perspective of energy, balconies are not desirable for residential buildings. However combined with glazing, balconies can achieve an energy surplus, interestingly this is especially the case when they are situated on the northern side.

Building zoo

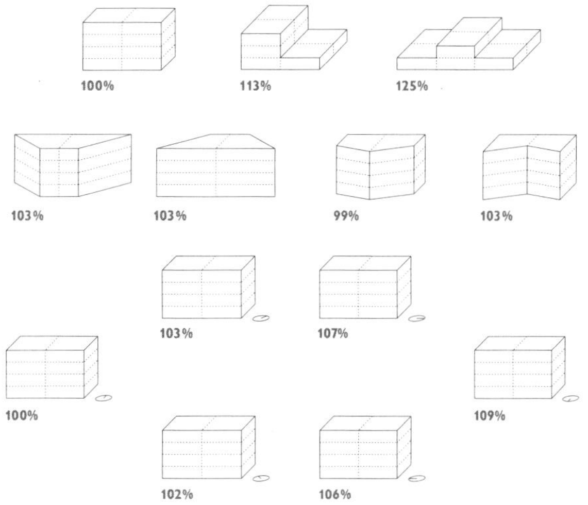

Total primary energy n.r.
in relation to the basic version

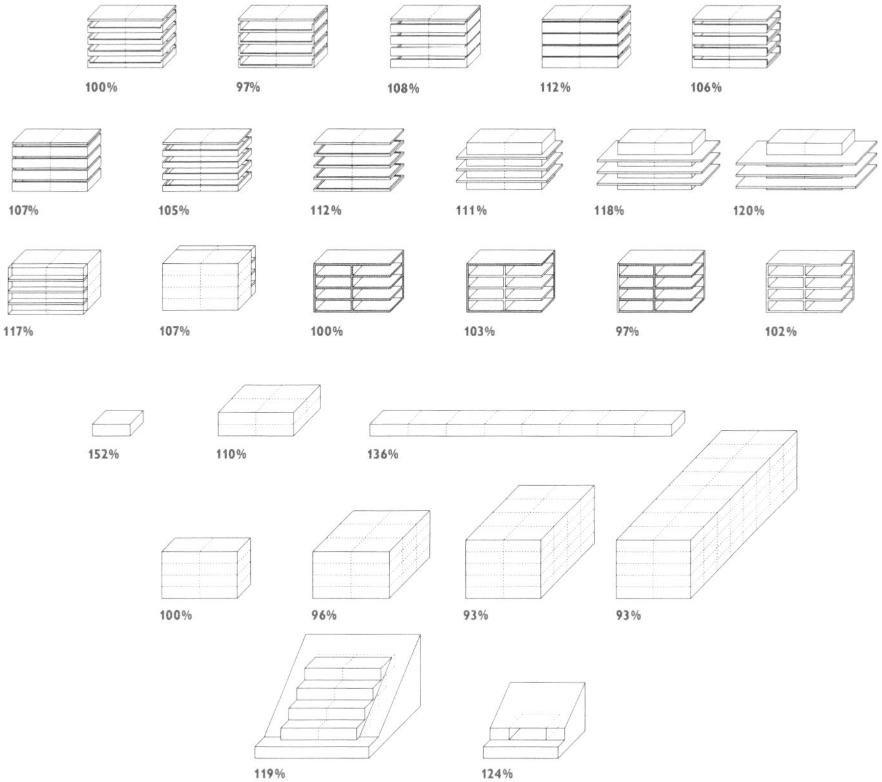

Gion Caminada – Climate and Behaviour

Mankind is not only a rational entity, but also a physical being. It takes the dialectic interaction between understanding and feelings guided by the senses to produce an environment that is compatible with humans. Emotions, events – both recurring and unique – and even coincidences interacting with elementary invariables enhance living.

Every architectural intervention attempts to create such living spaces. Their protagonists therefore require great competence. That can only be achieved if architecture does not surrender to card-carrying specialists. The field's core competence is mastering space. Architects are more than generalists who administrate knowledge and delegate technical problems to specialists.

Limited resources and climate change are forcing us to act. To achieve promising change, we must regain our self-assurance and trust in ourselves. It is the core task of architecture to create places that give people support and hope. The global way of building has contributed to a loss of location. That is due to technological advances, but is also of our own (cultural) making. Former limits on the availability of building materials and technical means led to the stable cultures and spaces that we value so greatly today. The positive effects of such limitation cannot be forced upon us in today's circumstances. But I firmly believe that cultural processes can move in a similar direction – towards strong ideas and narrative connections that revitalize aspects of authenticity and identity.

In view of climate change and energy problems, recovering the nature of a location and making it count can be regarded as a new opportunity. Grasping climate as a design factor provides us with old-new parameters.

In addition to the efficiency that improved technology aims for, self-sufficiency plays an important role in architecture to examine the limits of our behaviour. Of course people should not fall behind their status of civilisation. That is why designers must succeed in convincing them for instance that different temperature zones do not mean a lack of comfort, but instead open up new living qualities.

That concept is not principally aimed at a better person. It is not about returning to nature, but instead much more about allowing people to discover a broad range of phenomena that can enrich the way we live on this planet. A newly grasped nature-culture relationship that can break down the current dichotomy may be the right way forward. It is a direction that mediates between mindfulness and appropriation at the

same time. Creating identities where responsibility can be inspired must be the key theme for future ideas. Places that allow a high degree of identity are far more valuable than merely their aesthetic enjoyment: They can communicate to people that they belong to a society. That kind of identity is not produced by architecture that always aims to be object-based. On the contrary, it can only be achieved through conscious building that is based on collective agreement.
An active approach to design that is able to handle climate aspects as a design factor could also lead to tradition again becoming a serious and true concern of architecture. Tradition is no more – and yet no less – than the reflection of what has stood the test of time and space.

Example: The Terrihütte
The extension for the SAC hut on the Greina plateau had the aim of being distinct from our daily locations on the valley floor. At the same time, it also manifests the SAC members' political resistance to today's building practice. The section members of SAC Terri painstakingly gathered stones in the countryside. The Greina region mainly consists of stones, meadows, water and the horizon. We wanted to implement a meaningful idea. Expressed in facts and figures, the hut probably did not take less energy to build than if we had flown in the material from the valley. But having that factor as the only guideline would not have satisfied our cultural demands. Equally, the energy debate cannot merely have the aim of efficiency. It is hoped that we created something that outlasts the zeitgeist and with its special form of sustainability stands above the mere task of cost-minimising.

Conclusion

Our thesis reveals that the impulse of Modernism – the ability to export the ideal house type that is independent of its location and therefore independent of the local climate – is an imperialist approach. As much as this way of thinking appeared to be enlightened at the time, it is based on a capitalist world view that exploits resources globally, but only makes them locally available to a few.

Even if we believe we have stylistically moved on from Modernism, technology seems to remain an unchanged panacea in the buildings themselves. We should therefore replace our hysteria of cutting the cord from Modernism with a return to regarding history as a continuous, uninterrupted development of architecture and technology – especially if we wish to survive together. We can learn from autochthonous building methods that have steadily improved over long periods of time. It is how empirical knowledge has been accrued, passed on to the next generation and constantly optimised. In our fast moving times, which define individual invention as the measure of all things and celebrate high profile presentations, that knowledge has been ignored. It seems to have been permanently lost. To take an integral view of today's complex situations with respect to increasingly demanding energy efficiency and sustainability requirements into account, we therefore need a potent instrument – simulation. It can, if only partially, replace and perhaps even optimise lost empirical knowledge. The original experiences were based on long-term experiment, as insight could only be gained from constructed buildings. Today, it is possible to use simulation to present a design hypothesis at an early developmental stage. The process resembles accelerated natural selection. It can provide an approximation of the expected reality.

Simulation clearly shows designers the leverage of individual measures. In this way, alternatives in the formulation of our buildings can be offered with respect to energy consumption and generation. The aim is to optimise as lean an operation as possible for the later building at an early design stage. To close the cycle, the simulated data should be tested on the erected building so that the calculating model can be further optimized. Thanks to its high degree of efficiency, it is hoped that the early planning process can be slowed down in this way, since it is important to patiently consider the climatic conditions, allowing one to react to them more flexibly. Taking the climate and therefore the location into account is not only necessary from an energy perspective: Culture and climate cannot be separated. Our perception and comfort demands are decisively shaped by the climatic conditions we live in. So an integral, simultaneous grasp of culture, lifestyle, climate and architecture must supplement the technical simulation.

Architecture is always holistic. System engineers and architects should therefore dare to hold initial meetings together. The automated process of "first architecture, then technology" must be interrupted. Technology is no longer something that is subsequently installed to make the architecture work. If it is taken into account at an early project stage, the simulated design process also shifts the stationary view on architecture as lifeless, merely well-proportioned matter, towards a dynamic organism that is able to react to the environment in a differentiated way.

Perhaps this path will lead to fewer works of genius, but it can produce architecture that is once again well founded and consolidated, with a great social relevance. The value addition chain between empiricism, science, clarity and usability would ideally be continuous. And in the best cases, artistic intuition, architectural intention and scientific spirit could join forces – to allow climate to become a design factor.

Alder, Michael and Vogt, Klaus: Energiesparhaus in Muttenz BL. In: Archithese Nr. 4. Zurich 1981. p. 26–27

Banham, Reyner: Die Architektur der wohl-temperierten Umwelt, German 1st edition. In: Arch + 93, Aachen: February 1988

Behling, Sophia and Stefan (Eds.): Solar Power, The Evolution of Sustainable Architecture. Munich: Prestel, 2000

Bosch, J., Kittinger, A., Karamuk, Ü., Richter, J., Prima, Urs: Boba Fett. Project competition, Bernerstrasse Zurich (2nd Phase). March 2002

Brunner, Ernst, Schweizerische Gesellschaft für Volkskunde (Ed.): Die Bauernhäuser im Kanton Luzern. Lucerne: Kantonaler Lehrmittelverlag, 1977

Chadirji, Rifat: Concepts and Influences. Towards a Regionalized International Architecture. London: KPI Limited, 1986

Cohen J. L., Olsberg N., Escher F., Nicholas Olsberg (Ed.): Between Earth and Heaven – The Architecture of John Lautner. New York: Rizzoli International Publications Inc., 2008. In collaboration with the Hammer Museum Los Angeles

Corrodi, Michelle, Spechtenhauser, Klaus: LichtEinfall. ETH Wohnforum, Departement Architektur. Basel/Boston/Berlin: Birkhäuser, 2008

Fathy, Hassan: Architektur aus 1001 Steinen. In: Arch + 88 Aachen: February 1987

Gisel, Ernst: Ferienhaus eines Architekten auf Rigi-Kaltbad. In: Werk Nr. 4. Zurich 1960. p. 126

Gropius, Walter: Internationale Architektur. Munich: Albert Langen 1925

Hegger M., Fuchs M., Stark T., Zeumer M.: Energieatlas: Nachhaltige Architektur. Basel: Birkhäuser, 2007

Hoesli, Bernhard: Architektur lehren, gta ETH Hönggerberg. Zurich, 1989

Hasan-Uddin, Khan (Ed.), Correa, Charles: Architect in India. New York: Butterworth Architecture, 1987

Joedicke, Jürgen (Ed.): Candilis Josic Woods. Ein Jahrzehnt Architektur und Stadtplanung. Stuttgart/Bern: Karl Krämer, 1968

Johnson, Philip C., Hitchcock, Henry-Russell: The International Style: Architecture Since 1922. Museum of Modern Art. New York: publication and exhibition, 1932

Konstantinidis, Aris: Heutige Architektur und anonymes Bauen. In: Heft Baumeister 4/1965, Thema, Schulen; Wohnhäuser. Munich: Callwey 1965, p. 416–418

Krausse, Joachim: Im Gespräch. In: Arch + 126, Solare Architektur, Aachen: April 1995, p. 22–25

Krausse J., Lichtenstein C. (Ed.): Your Private Sky – R. Buckminster Fuller, Baden: Lars Müller, 1999

Krausse, Joachim (Ed.): Richard Buckminster Fuller. Bedienungsanleitung für das Raumschiff Erde – und andere Schriften. Hamburg: Philo Fine Arts/EVA Europäische Verlagsanstalt, 2008

Luchsinger, Christoph: High-Tech als Low-Tech. In: werk, bauen + wohnen Nr. 1/2. Zurich 1998. p. 36

Metz, Karl H.: Ursprünge der Zukunft. Die Geschichte der Technik in der westlichen Zivilisation, Paderborn: Verlag Ferdinand Schöningh, 2006

Mörsch, Georg: Kulturverschwendung. In: tec 21 Nr. 45, Ökologie und Baukultur. Zurich 2008. p. 30–32

Nachtigall, Werner: Bau-Bionik. Natur, Analogien, Technik. Berlin: Springer, 2003

Norberg-Schulz, Christian: Genius Loci. Landschaft, Lebensraum, Baukunst. Stuttgart: Klett-Cotta, 1982

Paillard, Claude: Terrassenhaus in Zürich-Witikon. In: Werk Nr. 2. Zurich 1961. p. 55

Reinhard, Hans and Gret: Methode für Besonnungsbestimmung. In: Werk Nr. 3. Zurich 1949. p. 72–74

Rieben, Samuel: Ein Ingenieur der Wärmetechnik bespricht die Fragen der vorgehängten Fassade, der Klimatisation, der Heizung, der Energielösung. In: Werk Nr. 4. Zurich 1974. p. 430

Rowe, Colin, Koetter, Fred: Collage City. Basel, Boston, Stuttgart: Birkhäuser, 1984

Sabady, Pierre R.: Haus und Sonnenkraft. Zurich: Helion (2nd edition) 1976. p. 20

Sabady, Pierre R.: Biosolar-Architektur. In: Werk/Archithese Nr. 19–20 (July/August). Zurich 1978. p. 18

Scherer, Hans Ulrich: Terrassenbauten. In: Werk Nr. 6. Zurich 1966. p. 201

Schwarz, Dietrich: Nachhaltiges Bauen. In: Detail Nr. 6, Energieeffiziente Architektur 2007

Spreng, Daniel, Semadeni, Marco: Energie, Umwelt und die 2000-Watt-Gesellschaft. Zurich: Centre for Energy Policy and Economics CEPE, ETH, 2001

Stierlin, Henri: Im Spiegel der Energiekrise. In: Werk Nr. 4. Zurich 1974. p. 416

Taut, Bruno: Das japanische Haus und sein Leben. Manfred Speidel (Ed.). 4th edition, Berlin: Gebr. Mann, 2005

Watsuji, Tetsuro: Fudo – Wind und Erde. Der Zusammenhang zwischen Klima und Kultur, Darmstadt: Wissenschaftliche Buchgesellschaft, Darmstadt 1992

Ungers, Oswald Mathias: Sieben Variationen des Raumes über die Sieben Leuchter von John Ruskin. Stuttgart: Gerd Hatje, 1985

Vetsch, Peter: Erd- und Höhlenhäuser von Peter Vetsch. Sulgen: Niggli 1994

Von Vegesack, A., Kries M.: Leben unter dem Halbmond – Die Wohnkulturen der arabischen Welt. Vitra Design Stiftung, 2nd edition. Weil am Rhein, 2007

Wagner, Martin: Das wachsende Haus. Ein Beitrag zur Lösung der städtischen Wohnungsfrage. Berlin, 1932

Wassmer, Markus, Fischer, Florian, Zbinden, Ueli: Wechselseitig. Zu Architektur und Technik. Munich: Verlag Technische Universität 2006

Wirz, Heinz (Ed.): Bearth & Deplazes. Konstrukte. Lucerne: Quart, 2005

Würtenberger, Franzsepp: Die Architektur der Lebenwesen. Info. Karlsruhe: Verlagsgesellschaft, 1989

Zophoniasson-Baierl, Ulrike (Ed.): Michael Alder. Das Haus als Typ. Basel/Boston/Berlin: Birkhäuser, 2006

Contributors

Christian Hönger

Born in 1959, graduate architect ETH BSA SIA. From 1991 architectural office giuliani.hönger with Lorenzo Giuliani in Zurich (www.giulianihoenger.ch). Assistant at the ETH Zurich, Lecturer at the FHNW Basel, 2005 Professor at the HSLU – T&A, 2005–08 conception, direction, accreditation of the MA course in Architecture. From 2008, research on "Climate as a Design Factor", "A Liveable Window", and "The Building Shell – A Decision-Making Tool". MA 2012 autumn semester focus: "Structure", publication: "Structure – Precarious Speculation".

Tina Unruh

Born in 1971, graduate architect NDS ETH gta. Since 2000, buildings, projects and texts with Patric Unruh in Zurich and Hamburg. Assistant at the ETH. Development and Direction of the Competence Centre Material, Structure & Energy in Architecture at the HSLU – T&A, 2006–2012. Lecturer in the MA course since 2009. Work on fields including "Researching Architecture". Editor of the Laboratorium series, Quart Verlag, Lucerne.

Urs-Peter Menti

Born in 1969, graduate engineer ETH/SIA. Studied Mechanical Engineering at the ETH Zurich. From 1995 onwards Senior Consultant at Amstein + Walthert in Zurich. Since 2004 at the Lucerne University of Applied Sciences and Arts – Engineering & Architecture. Initially Research Assistant, since 2008 full-time Lecturer in Building Technology and Head of the Centre for Integral Building Technology (ZIG). Professor since 2010. Research and consulting work in the fields of sustainable building, energy and building technology, and simulation.

Christoph Stettler

Born in 1988, BSc in Building Technology HLK. 2003 to 2007 Building Technology Planner: Ventilation. Since 2012 Assistant at the Centre for Integral Building Technology (ZIG) at the Lucerne University of Applied Sciences and Arts – Engineering & Architecture. Responsible for simulation in the field of energy optimization and sustainable building, as well as for the planning and supervision of laboratory experiments for training and further education.

Roman Brunner

Born in 1976, graduate architect FH, art historian MA, 2002–2005 freelance architect, 2004–2010 studied History of Art and Philosophy at the University of Bern, 2004–07 Teaching Assistant and 2007–2010 Research Assistant as the HSLU – T&A for research on "Climate as a Design Factor" and "A Liveable Window". Since 2010 monument preservation in the Canton of Zug.

Christoph Wieser

Born in 1967, graduate architect ETH, Dr. sc., Architectural Theoretician. Studied in Zurich and Lausanne, postgraduate studies in History and Theory of Architecture at the gta, ETHZ, Ph. D. at the ETH Lausanne in 2005, Assistant and Lecturer at the ETHZ. Editor of the magazine bauen+wohnen 2003–09. Since 2006 Lecturer in the MA Architecture course at the Zurich University of Applied Sciences in Winterthur; ibid. Head of the Centre of Structural Design 2009–13, numerous publications.

Born in 1971, researching architect, Dr. sc. ETH. Research focuses: Non-European house building, ethnographic architectural research, construction theory. 2004–2010 Research Assistant under Professor Andrea Deplazes, ETH Zurich. Since 2011 Lecturer in Architecture and Construction, ETH Zurich. 2013 Senior Researcher at the Future Cities Laboratory (Singapur), ETH Zurich. Swiss Art Award 2012 (Category: Architecture) Publication: Weltkonstruktion. Der aussereuropäische Hausbau und die moderne Architektur. Ein Wissensinventar (Berlin 2013)

Sascha Roesler

Born in 1967 in Pully, Switzerland, works as an architect in Paris. In 2000, Philippe Rahm was awarded a Villa Medici scholarship. He participated in a series of exhibitions around the world, 2005–6 Principal of the Architectural Association School of Architecture in London and has since had various positions as Guest Professor and Lecturer. His office is currently working on several projects in Europe and Taiwan. Important publications: Physiological Architecture, Birkhäuser Verlag, 2002; Distortions, HYX, 2005, Environ(ne)ment: Approaches for Tomorrow, Skira, 2006, Architecture Météorologique, Archibooks, 2009.

Philippe Rahm

Born in 1964, graduate architect ETH BSA SIA. Since 1996, own architectural office in Zurich (www.boltshauser.info). Design Assistant under Peter Märkli at the ETH Zurich and EPFL Lausanne, Lecturer at the HTW Chur and Chur institute of architecture CIA. Important publications: Elementares zum Raum. Roger Boltshauser Werke, Springer Verlag Vienna, 2009; Haus Rauch, Birkhäuser Verlag, 2010 and Roger Boltshauser – Transformator, Architektur Galerie Berlin, 2012

Roger Boltshauser

Born in 1957 in Vrin, Switzerland. Trained as a carpenter. Vocational school in Zurich. Postgraduate studies in Architecture at the ETH Zurich. Architectural office in Vrin. Since 1998, Assistant Professor and Lecturer in Architecture and Design at the ETH in Zurich. Since 2008, Associate Professor of Architecture and Design at the ETH in Zurich.

Gion A. Caminada

Born in 1981, graduated in Physics at the University of Bern. 2009, Ph.D. with a dissertation on climate and environmental physics at the University of Bern. From 2009 onwards, Research Assistant at the University of Bern in the field of Climate and Environmental Physics. Since 2010, Research Assistant at the Centre for Integral Building Technology, Lucerne University of Applied Sciences and Arts – Engineering & Architecture: Research and consulting work in the field of sustainable building, energy and building technology, and simulation.

Dieter Lüthi

Financial and conceptual support

Special thanks to the institutions and sponsoring companies that provided financial support, which was an essential factor in the publication of this series. Such cultural engagement enhances the fruitful, friendly collaboration between construction culture and the building industry. Thank you for your cooperation.

Amt für Hochbauten der Stadt Zürich
Fachstelle Nachhaltiges Bauen

Eduard Truninger AG, Zürich

GKP Fassadentechnik AG, Aadorf

Martinelli + Menti AG, Luzern

Laboratorium

Laboratorium: A study environment in which to reflect, but above all to work and experiment. It is not just for testing, but also for presenting ideas and theories, in brief – a place of research. Because laborare not only means "to work", but also "to make an effort" and is therefore an activity with an open end and related to research.

Edited by: Lucerne University of Applied Sciences and Arts – School of Engineering and Architecture, Tina Unruh

Volume 1: Climate as a Design Factor
New edition German: ISBN 978-3-03761-072-5
New edition English: ISBN 978-3-03761-073-2

Volume 2: Researching Architecture
German ISBN 978-3-03761-019-0
English ISBN 978-3-03761-023-7

Volume 3: Spatial Thinking
German ISBN 978-3-03761-041-1
English ISBN 978-3-03761-055-8

Quart Verlag GmbH, Heinz Wirz
CH-6006 Luzern
books@quart.ch, www.quart.ch